Mirrors

© 2023 by University of Louisiana at Lafayette Press
All rights reserved
ISBN 13 (paper): 978-1-946160-96-6

http://ulpress.org
University of Louisiana at Lafayette Press
P.O. Box 43558
Lafayette, LA 70504-3558

cover art by Lily Sage Cosby

Printed in the United States

Library of Congress Cataloging-in-Publication Data
Names: Armand, David, 1980- author.
Title: Mirrors : and other reflections / by David Armand.
Description: Lafayette, LA : University of Louisiana at Lafayette Press,
    [2022]
Identifiers: LCCN 2022047043 | ISBN 9781946160966 (paperback)
Subjects: LCSH: Armand, David, 1980---Childhood and youth. | Authors,
    American--21st century--Biography. | LCGFT: Autobiographies. | Essays.
Classification: LCC PS3601.R55 Z46 2022 | DDC 813/.6 [B]--dc23/
eng/20221121
LC record available at https://lccn.loc.gov/2022047043

Mirrors

and other reflections

By David Armand

UNIVERSITY OF LOUISIANA AT LAFAYETTE PRESS
2023

Table of Contents

Acknowledgments

Grateful acknowledgment is made to the editors of the following journals in which some of these essays originally appeared, sometimes in slightly different form.

"Adoption" *as* "My First Game Console: Nintendo Entertainment System" (*Hobart*)

"Drivers Ed" (*The McNeese Review*)

"Ghosts in the Mountains" (*Fiction Southeast*)

"Intro: Hiraeth" *as* "On Fairs and Longing in Louisiana" (*Southbound*)

"Independence Day, Part One" (*Deep South Magazine*)

"Independence Day, Part Two" (*Opossum*)

"Mirrors" (*Belmont Story Review*)

"Real Work" (*Drafthorse*)

"Still Life of an Old Library in Folsom, Louisiana" (*Louisiana Libraries*)

"Truants" (*Level: Deepsouth*)

for my father

"The Son can do nothing of himself,
but what he seeth the Father do:
for what things soever he doeth,
these also doeth the Son likewise."
—John 5:19

"'Son,' she said, 'Have I got a little story for you.'"
—Pearl Jam

Intro
Hiraeth

When I was a kid, one of the few salves for the end of the summer and the beginning of another long school year was going to the St. Tammany Parish Fair in Covington, Louisiana.

There was always that sense of anticipation and excitement as the weather cooled and eased into fall, the days growing shorter, a feeling that things were changing.

I remember being off school on opening day, the parade that marshaled it in with its streamered floats and high school marching bands, how the rides and booths had seemingly gone up overnight, filling the dusty, hay-strewn fairgrounds with their lights and music and the din of commerce, only for it to all be gone a few days later.

We always started in the livestock exhibit, the sweet smell of hay and manure and animal sweat filling the still air of the cinderblock barn, a few metal fans turning lazily overhead. I knew a couple of kids from school who were in 4-H, and I would see them standing next to a calf or a potbellied pig or a large golden rooster, its waxy feathers glistening in the dusty light. The judges would go around with their wooden clipboards and place blue ribbons next to the best ones.

After that, we walked out onto the midway, where you could hear the metal-on-metal skirl of the rides, the sounds of gears and well-oiled chains as bright, colorful cars moved over steel tracks and their riders screamed in delight, or maybe it was terror. There were the bumper cars, the Gravitron, the Ferris wheel.

I remember all of that. And I remember the tanned leathery skin of the men behind the wooden booths—the carnival barkers—and how they beckoned us over with a palmful of plastic darts. You could throw them at a balloon on a corkboard wall, they said, and win a stuffed animal that was dangling from a drooping clothesline. One time, I won a knife that you could slip into a leather case and clip to your belt.

There was a sense of magic about it all: the things people make and do so that they can come together and spend time around each other, how we take in all these experiences to have something worth remembering and thinking about later.

But many years have passed since then, too many to count, and so I come back to this same fair with my own family, my wife and two kids, where there's this feeling of what the Welsh call *hiraeth*, a nostalgia that's so deep it creeps through your bones.

And part of me wants to be that kid again, to remember when everything had the sheen of being new and life felt comfortingly overwhelming. So I look down at my children, the lights glistening in their eyes, their hands sticky with cotton candy, and I can almost be there. Almost. And somehow that's close enough.

*

What follows is a collection of interconnected essays, told somewhat chronologically, but each piece should be able to stand on its own as well—like a collection of short stories. I wanted to think of this book as though it were a concept album, like Pink Floyd used to put out, with an intro, a coda, and a "part one" and "part two" to one of the essays.

Lastly, while each of these pieces is true to my own personal memory of the events described, the names of some of the people involved have been changed. I also refer to my adoptive family as my stepparents and stepsiblings throughout the book, mainly for clarity's sake—though in real life I grew up calling them my mom and dad, my brother and sisters.

Adoption

My wife and kids and I are driving around in New Orleans, not too far from where I spent the first years of my life and then the occasional week during the summer when I stayed with my grandmother when I was a kid, and I'm telling them how I believe one of the most important things we have is our memory, the images and associations from our childhoods, and how driving through this city today sends my own memories hurtling back at me like buckshot.

But everything here seems so different now: the abandoned houses, pocked with graffiti and boarded up with sheets of dark and moldy plywood. Windows smashed and broken, roofs caved in, a frayed blue tarp gently flapping in the warm breeze. Then there are the weeded lots where a house once was, the hood or trunk of a forgotten car emerging like a hand from a rising river. *Save me*, it seems to say.

Almost fourteen years since the waters came through and still so much wreckage. It makes for a strange connection to your past. To see what was once so familiar, now lost.

But I can still remember those far-off summers in New Orleans. It was 1988 and I had just gotten my first game console, a Nintendo Entertainment System. It came with one gray cartridge that had both *Super Mario Bros.* and *Duck Hunt* on it, two small rectangular controllers with red and black buttons that fit perfectly in my eight-year-old hand, and a Zapper gun so you could shoot skeet and kill a passel of ducks if you wanted to. If you missed, a little brown dog would come out of the weeds and snicker at you.

I had a small TV that I hooked my Nintendo up to and would sit on the floor for hours playing games like *The Legend of Zelda, Castlevania, Double Dragon, Excitebike, Mike Tyson's Punch-Out!!*, and *Ikari Warriors*.

And for at least one week during each summer before they moved out of the city and to Folsom so they could be closer to us, I would stay with my grandparents at their house off Paris Avenue in New Orleans. This was the same house in which I had lived my first couple of years before being adopted by an aunt and uncle after my mother could no longer take care of me.

I loved going there, despite some of the bad memories of my mother screaming and locking herself in her room for hours, disappearing altogether for days, even weeks, at a time, leaving me for someone else to take care of.

Maybe it was to make up for these things, or maybe it was to assuage any guilt she may have had for not raising me herself, my grandmother would make those weekly stays almost magical for me. I would cart my Nintendo along with me, where I would hook it up to a little TV in what we called the playroom, the same room where I had lived as a baby before being adopted. It still had the same blue carpet, the same NASA logo on the door that my uncle had painted when he lived in there as a teenager, the same hardened crescent of skin on the door where he had super-glued his thumb just above the knob and had to slice it off with a straight razor and then paint over it so his parents wouldn't know what he had done while they were asleep.

There was still the same darkened window that looked out onto the garage where my grandfather kept his workshop tools for carving decoys and where my uncle still kept old car parts and tools for when he operated a repair shop out of there. The window was partially covered with a metal shelf and table, and I never liked to look out of it for fear I would see something beyond the moted shadows, which shifted and bent with the light. Nor did I want to see my own ghostly reflection in the window's dusty surface. So I kept the wooden shutters inside the room closed and latched.

My family would say that house was haunted: chairs sometimes sliding across the kitchen floor, a door creaking open on its hinges, whispers coming from empty rooms. Images of people long dead hovering outside the kitchen window, translucent and wavering in the gloom. And even though I never saw any of these things, my imagination made them real enough.

Still, I would spend hours sitting on the floor alone, playing Nintendo or sometimes reading old Nancy Drew mysteries that had once belonged to my mother. I would imagine her in this same room reading these same books, and I would wonder about where she was. Was she thinking about me? Did she have things of mine that she would look at to remind her of my life before she had given me away?

I remember there was an old Pac-Man mini game console in the closet that my mother had gotten for me when I still lived there with her. It was made in the shape of Pac-Man's head and the tiny screen was where his eyes should have been. The little orange buttons let you move him up and down a maze so that he could eat those pixelated white dots along the way and kill all those roaming ghosts before they could devour him—or whatever it was they did. I would play this for hours too, and I can still remember the warm plastic under my hands, how it smelled after it got really warm, the coppery tang of the batteries inside.

My mother had taken me to what we called "the dime store" and bought it for me, against the advice of the cashier who had said I was too young for it, but I played that console until it stopped working. I loved being in that room, being at my grandmother's house for a whole week—no school, no chores, being doted on like when I was really young.

During the day sometimes and after lunch, my grandmother would take me to Toys "R" Us and let me pick out a new Nintendo game or a GI Joe. Other days she would take me to the arcade and let me pump a fistful of quarters into the machines, playing the larger, more exciting versions of the games I had back at home. She took me to Storyland at City Park, where I could climb the old fairy-tale-inspired sculptures, sit right in the mouth of the great whale from Pinocchio. My mother used to take me there too, before she stopped being able to see me altogether.

Still, these were some of the best times I had in my childhood.

I was able to shut out the world back then. It was like pulling a thick, dark curtain over all that was going on outside that little magical 8-bit universe that I seemed to inhabit. And, believe me, there was a lot going on, a lot for me to shut out. These are the things that are hard to talk about with my kids—who themselves are only thirteen and ten—as we drive around the city, looking at everything, and me telling them all about what once was.

I remember the social worker who came to check on me once. We were living in a rented single-wide trailer in Folsom, about two hours north of New Orleans. I was in fourth grade.

The social worker's name was Mrs. Snow. As I sat in my older stepsister's room playing a Nintendo game I had rented called *Faxanadu*, Mrs. Snow talked to my stepparents in the den.

"Does David seem to be adjusting?" she said. "Does he have any friends, does he make good grades in school?"

In the game I was playing, your character was some sort of wizard-looking guy and you had to walk through a medieval village, talking to shopkeepers and other tradesmen so that you could build up your inventory to save the townspeople and their homes.

Then, I heard Mrs. Snow ask my stepparents, "Would it be all right if I talked to him?"

"Sure," my stepdad said. Then they called me out to where they were sitting. I paused the game and put down my controller.

"Hi, David," Mrs. Snow was saying to me as I walked into the room. She stood up from where she had been sitting next to my stepparents on the sofa and shook my hand. She was wearing a bright red pantsuit and had hair that was so blond it looked almost white in that thick shaft of light that slanted in through the curtainless window and that looked out into a large field bordered by a wall of woods behind our trailer.

Living out in the country, among horse pastures and rolling fields pocked with ponds and oak trees, was nothing like the city. It was almost like living in one of those fairy tales from Storyland. And this social worker was almost like one of its characters.

"My name's Mrs. Snow," she said.

"Hi," I said. I searched the tiny room for something to focus on so I didn't have to make eye contact with this woman whom I had never met, whose purpose for being there I didn't quite understand. After all, I was only eight years old.

"Are you happy here, David?" Mrs. Snow asked.

"Yes, ma'am."

"Good," she said. "Do you like where you go to school?"

"Yes."

"Good," she said again. "That's all very, very good to hear."

I didn't say anything. My stepparents just watched us from their spot on the sofa.

"Well, I won't keep you any longer," Mrs. Snow told me. "I know you've probably got plenty of things you'd rather be doing than talking to me. It was nice meeting you, David."

"You too," I said. Then I went back to my stepsister's room and unpaused my game.

*

As I got older and my adoption was finalized, my stepdad fell deeper and deeper into alcoholism, eventually losing his job so that I had to drop out of school and work full-time to help support my adoptive family. I had mostly lost interest in Nintendo by then and had moved from that console to a Sega Genesis and then finally to a PlayStation. I would play games like *Tomb Raider* and *Grand Theft Auto* until two or three in the morning those days, all after working night shifts as a phone operator and then on a production line in a flag printing factory. Those were difficult times but at least I had something that helped get me through them. Always a place I could go to escape.

I still went to the arcade sometimes, a small square behind the food court of the local shopping mall, where kids played *Street Fighter* or *Mortal Kombat*, placing their quarters on top of the console to hold their place in line. But there was an element of danger in those darkened places now, something that I hadn't noticed when I was younger, or maybe it simply wasn't there when the games hadn't been so violent and bloody.

When I was in high school, they turned what was once a Kenny Rogers Roasters into a small video arcade, and I can remember a couple of my friends and I going there and buying some valium from some guy in a back room where they kept the air hockey table, the fluorescent black light tube overhead making our skin glow and our teeth a purplish-white color as he handed us the little pills from his sweaty palm.

It felt like something out of an after-school special. But we were bored and had been looking for something to do.

"Y'all want to buy some coke, too?" he said after putting the money we had given him in his jacket pocket.

I looked over at my friend Gary.

"Do you want to?" I asked him.

"Yeah, let's get it," he said.

"Cool," was all that other guy said before producing a tiny little bag full of white powder. It shimmered under the light.

I gave him the money and put the drugs in my pocket and then walked through the arcade, past a row of games I was no longer interested in playing, hadn't been for several years—having discovered a new escape, another way to push away the time and those terrible feelings that it carried with it on its shoulders.

We drove around all night, going up and down gravel roads that cut through the trailer park where one of my friends lived—and where I would eventually stay for a while after moving away from home one night when I saw my stepdad choke my stepmom for what I had decided would be the last time.

We had each done a couple of lines of coke that night, but my friends had also taken the valium, so they didn't really feel the drug like I was experiencing it. I hadn't taken any pills so was getting the full effects of the cocaine. I felt invincible, and I remember thinking that if I accidentally flipped my truck over in one of the steep ditches that lined the road, I'd easily be able to lift it back out and set it right again. It was an incredible feeling, but one I knew even then was false. And dangerous.

When the sun started to come up, I parked in my friend's yard and tried to sleep in the damp bed of the truck, the corrugated surface digging into my legs and back, making it impossible to doze off even if I hadn't done all that coke earlier. I watched the sun come up over the black skeletons of pine trees instead. I could smell woodsmoke in the distance. Someone burning trash in their yard.

Then, I grew up, thankfully shedding all of those bad habits and starting a family of my own. Hoping to break the curses of my own past, my own bad decisions.

I've since bought a new Nintendo as well, but it's not an original one. In fact, it's more like a homemade console with hundreds of games preloaded onto it. Some of them I've never even heard of, but a good bit of them are just the same as the ones I remember playing as a kid. Of course, it's not completely the same. It will never be like coming home from school and running up the gravel driveway as the bus pulls off in a cloud of dark exhaust, grabbing a snack from the kitchen before retreating to my room and that underground world of plumbers and pipes and mushrooms and dangerously shifting clouds.

Sometimes I could hear my stepparents fighting in the other room, yelling about the lack of money, how they weren't going to be able to pay the bills that month, about how my stepdad spent too much time going out to bars every night, the DWIs he was racking up. He had lost his license but still continued to drive anyway. He kept a sawed-off shotgun under his seat in the car wherever he went. I'm not making this up. My stepmom said they wouldn't let him out of jail the next time. He just said she was crazy. Then he'd leave again.

But eventually, I wouldn't even hear those old arguments anymore. It would just be me and the game scrolling across the tiny TV screen in my bedroom, a game I might have rented earlier that week from the little video store in town, where you had to take the case for the game you wanted up to the counter and then wait as the person working there would retrieve the actual cartridge from a shelf behind the desk. He'd put an "Out on Rental" tag on the case and then write your information down on a yellow index card. It took a few minutes, but the time waiting was somehow—like everything else in childhood seems—magical and worth the simple pleasure of the experience itself.

These are the stories I tell my children as we drive through this semi-ruined city—though I certainly don't tell them all of it—the place where I once lived and played and fretted and cried and experienced joy. Even though now it is nothing like it used to be. The house where I spent the first couple of years of my life, the place I like to think formed such a large part of who I am today, is not even there anymore.

After being flooded by the hurricane, then slowly repaired (the orange spray-painted X with its symbols of who died there or not were on the outside wall for months before finally being covered over), and then more years of neglect, its new owner lived in a FEMA trailer in the driveway where my grandmother used to park her car before ultimately giving up on the house altogether. (Once I went there and knocked on the door to ask if I could look around, to tell him that I used to live there as a kid and would love to walk inside, but he just stood at the door and looked me up and down before turning me away. I didn't persist, especially after seeing the .45 at his side. Like everyone else, he had already been through too much. Why would he have trusted me, believed that my intentions to come inside were true?)

I had just wanted to see where I grew up, even though it had been damaged beyond my recognition. But now, like so many other things, the house is gone, demolished to make way for a new structure, a day care center according to the colorful sign out front where my grandfather used to cut the lawn, just under the oak tree where we used to park when we would visit after moving away, my car door once getting stuck on the oak's large roots and my stepdad having to get back in the driver's seat and pull the car up a bit on the road to get the door loose. I remember how mad he was.

And that Nintendo I played as a kid is probably in an attic somewhere now, and I'll never see it again. So are all the games I played, the hours of joy trapped in those gray plastic cartridges, the escape from what had been going on outside of them. But those things are here now too and are with me as I drive around the city with my wife and my kids.

I don't tell them all of this, but they can probably pick up on what I'm thinking. A couple of times I have to wipe my eyes with my shirtsleeve. I see their faces in the rearview mirror looking at me as I drive around the potholes that are big enough for them to swim in, all the cracks in the street large enough to knock the axle off your car.

Nothing is the same here, I tell them. Not at all how it was when I was a kid. But then again, I say, what ever really is?

Independence Day, Part One

Growing up in rural Louisiana meant three things during the summer: the days were long, hot, and—if you were poor, like I was—boring. It seemed as though there was never anything to do. The days melted into each other so that time became somewhat amorphous, one long gulp of it that stretched like taffy, all the way from May until school started back up again in August. It was kind of like that Salvador Dali painting, all those drooping clocks in the desert.

To make things worse, my stepmom didn't have a car, and so we lived somewhat isolated in a single-wide trailer in the middle of a patch of cleared land, which was surrounded by thick pine woods. I remember spending the summer after I had just finished fourth grade clearing that little circle of land with my stepbrother, my stepdad, and my grandfather.

My stepdad had a machete, which he used to chop some of the smaller trees, branches, and all the growth that was webbed between them, knotted and stubborn. My grandfather, my stepbrother, and I followed behind him and picked up what he had cut, stuffing it inside a rusted-out wheelbarrow, then walked it all over to a pile we had made for burning.

Since most of the stuff my stepdad cut was green and wouldn't burn, my grandfather used a can of gasoline to get it going. It was late June, and everything was so hot and dry that the flames quickly spread beyond the bounds of the trash fire. They felt their way up the trees and high into the branches, where angry tendrils of flame whispered in the leaves, making them move as though a breeze was blowing. Thick, black plumes of smoke chuffed up into the cloudless blue sky overhead.

We dropped the wheelbarrow, the metal rakes, and the shovels we had been holding (our blistered and gloveless hands stinging with the heat and from our own sweat) and ran down the narrow trail we had cleared until we got to my stepdad's pickup truck. When he got behind the wheel, I could see that the hair on his arms, as well as his eyebrows, had been completely singed off.

My grandfather asked if we were all okay.

We just nodded our heads solemnly.

Then, my stepdad closed the door to the sweaty cab and muscled the truck down the narrow dirt lane, which we had cleared earlier that summer. We drove to the Jr. Food Mart in town to call the fire department. I remember my stepdad standing at the payphone and how the black plastic receiver quivered in his hand as he told them where our property was, the metal cord snaking around his red, sweaty arm as he talked and fidgeted.

"It's a mile up past the green light," I heard him say. We didn't have an address yet, so he had to give them landmarks. Then: "Yeah, right past the horse farm. On Verger Road."

We watched him as he lit a cigarette, then climbed back into the truck. My stepbrother and I were squeezed in the middle of the cab, right next to the gearshift. My grandfather was pressed up against the passenger door. The truck didn't have air-conditioning and his window was rolled down. He wasn't saying anything.

"You all right, Ed?" my stepdad asked him.

My grandfather didn't answer, probably because he hadn't even heard the question. He was deaf in his left ear.

Then my stepdad looked at my stepbrother and me. "Are y'all all right, boys?"

"Yeah," we said.

"Good."

He put the truck in reverse and backed out of the parking lot, the gearshift ramming into my leg as he did so. "Look," he said, "after the fire's out, we'll come back here, and I'll get y'all a cheeseburger."

"Okay," we said.

And that, I remember, ended up becoming the best part of that particular summer: eating cheeseburgers from the Jr. Food Mart after a long day's work—the thin aluminum foil wrappers with yellow writing on them to distinguish them from the regular hamburgers, whose packaging just had red lettering. The cool linoleum floor on your bare feet as you stood in line and watched the lady behind the counter take a pair of metal tongs and pull out from underneath the heat lamp whatever it was you had asked for. Potato logs, Cajun fries, fried chicken (which sometimes still had a stray white feather poking out from the crispy skin), hamburgers, cheeseburgers. All behind a fingerprint-smeared glass case on the counter. We washed the food down with large plastic bottles of Barq's root beer. Then we went back to work, cutting and burning.

*

By the end of that summer (and thanks in part to the brushfire we had accidentally started), we had a large patch of land cleared in the middle of the woods. And we were finally able to get a Bush Hog in there to finish the rest of the work. The path to get to the clearing was also wide enough now (and it had been covered with a half dozen dump truck loads of fresh white gravel) that our trailer could finally be delivered.

It was set up on cinder blocks, leveled (though not very well, as all the doors swung open on their hinges and, over the years, made holes in the thin walls behind them), and the tires were taken off, which my stepdad then sold to one of the workers—a sign that we weren't moving again any time soon. A well was dug, a septic tank was put into the ground, and the utility company came out and ran a single black line so we could get power. We spent the next fifteen years living in that trailer, clearing more land each summer, building a porch on it, a shed out back. My stepbrother and I would play in the woods. We made foxholes out of picnic table benches, shot each another with water guns. We built forts out of bales of hay, climbed trees, and rode our bikes over clay-hardened trails. My stepdad built a large vegetable garden out of a stack of creosote-covered railroad ties that he had found somewhere. When it rained, we swam in the creek that formed when a nearby pond overflowed its banks. Snakes skimmed its surface and rode the swift current into the dark woods beyond.

But then we grew up. And summers out there in the woods became more and more tedious. We didn't have cable TV, my stepmom still didn't have a car, and so my stepbrother and I would walk into Folsom to rent VHS tapes or Nintendo games from Movie World—a video store that was in a little, old house with creaking wooden floors and large windows, through which the sun slanted against the shelves on those long days leading up to the solstice, baking and fading the covers of the movie cases so that they looked as though someone had poured bleach on them.

We rented movies like *Lethal Weapon*, *Tango & Cash*, *Platoon*, *A Nightmare on Elm Street*. Violent movies. And the Nintendo games we picked out were no better. But it was summer, and we were bored. We had nothing else to do.

Sometimes we'd get snoballs for a dollar from the little stand next to where the old library used to be, which itself had once been a one-room shack where we used to go as kids to borrow books. I remember that library was so small that only three or four of us could go in at a time. We would hand the librarian our red laminated library card with our signature on it and she'd write our name and the date in a stained ledger she kept on her desk. Eventually, though, they built a new library on the other side of town. It was much bigger and air-conditioned.

My stepbrother and I had walked there one summer, just for something to do, to have a place to cool off, when a group of older kids approached us as we walked up the steps to go inside. They were skinny, dirty, their hair disheveled. They were barefoot.

"Y'all wanna fight?" one of them said. The others—varying in age, some boys, some girls—all laughed.

I thought they were kidding, until one of them pushed me. I like to think I was about to push him back, but, if I'm being completely honest here, I was more likely about to turn and run. Then the librarian, who must have been watching through the window, came outside and told them to leave.

They did. My stepbrother and I were allowed to go inside. But later, as we sat there looking at comic books and *Highlights* magazines, I saw those kids circling around the building, glaring in at us and making slicing motions across their necks with their dirty hands. There were more of them now, too, and some of them looked much, much older than us.

After a while, though, they finally gave up and left. It was getting dark, and my stepbrother and I went home just as the librarian was shutting off the lights and locking the doors. It was this kind of desperation that seemed to permeate everything we did during those long summer months. And the older we got, the more tangible that desperation seemed. Everyone was just bored, with nothing to do day after day after day. There was no two ways about it, as my stepdad would have said: people wanted to fight or otherwise get into trouble to ease the boredom.

And unfortunately, my stepbrother and I weren't an exception to that terrible fact. One night after my stepparents were asleep, we climbed out of the bedroom window and walked down the gravel shoulder alongside Highway 25, heading toward town. The high beams from the oncoming cars washed over us, their taillights becoming a single red point before finally disappearing over a crest in the road on their way to Franklinton, which was a bigger town just north of where we lived.

It was still humid out, even though the sun had been gone for hours, and the air was damp as we walked into town, its one red light blinking yellow now as we ambled past its soft glow toward Saia's, a small grocery store that we knew would be closed at that hour. It was an unspoken thing between us, but it felt as though we were just looking for trouble that night. That's how absolutely bored we had been.

My stepdad had told us stories of the things he had done as a boy when he was bored during the summer months: throwing water balloons into people's houses, tying together two garbage cans on either side of the road—using a length of thin string so that when a car passed through it, the string would pull taut, the metal cans slamming into the sides of the vehicle like battering rams. He also told us the stories of his own father and the welts he brought up on the boys' legs with his work belt after he had caught them causing trouble.

Despite this, and despite the fact that we knew my stepdad would take his belt to us if we were caught, my stepbrother and I walked behind the old grocery store to where a large forklift was parked next to a stack of flattened brown boxes. One of us climbed into the cab. The key was still in the ignition, but before we could start it, a voice came from somewhere in the darkness.

"Y'all get *outta* there!" it yelled. I couldn't tell from where the voice had materialized, but we both ran—over the pea gravel parking lot and eventually back home, where we climbed in the window and went to bed. There was nothing else to do.

*

As I got older and entered high school, the boredom of living in Folsom, Louisiana, seemed almost unbearable. Especially in the summer. It was no longer enough to rent movies, walk down the road at night, steal cigarettes from my stepdad, and smoke them in the woods. The tedium got worse and as a result, so did my behavior. It was a progression that seemed to create a sort of parallel, a parabola of cause and effect wherein more boredom equaled more trouble.

I started spending a lot of time at a friend's house. He lived near Covington, which was a slightly bigger town and therefore had slightly more to do. But this also meant there was more mischief for us to get into. We asked my friend's older sister to buy us cheap bottles of Mad Dog 20/20 from Winn-Dixie, which then progressed to us smoking pot, and, eventually, eating mushrooms, dropping acid, and—one time—snorting cocaine, which we bought from some kid at a video arcade.

I was sixteen then, and my stepdad had given my stepbrother and me his little Mazda B2200, the same one we had ridden in as kids to call the fire department from the Jr. Food Mart that time. It had so much mileage on it now that the odometer had already turned over to show all zeros, counting upward again from scratch, like a new moon waxing.

The hood of the truck was tied down with a stub of bungee cord, the bed was rusted out and dented, and the tailgate was gone. The bench seat inside was so torn and the vinyl so cracked that the yellow foam stuffing came out of the myriad tears like the insulation that our dogs constantly pulled out from under our trailer. I covered the seat with an old blanket. I even put some speakers from my room in there, wired them up to a cassette player that I stuck into the console so we could listen to music: Jane's Addiction, Faith No More, Red Hot Chili Peppers.

My stepbrother didn't have his license yet, so I mostly got to take the truck whenever I wanted. My friends and I would pile into it, some of them riding in the back, and we'd drive down the highway until we spotted some cow pastures with a good amount of woods around them. I'd find a place to park so that no one could see the truck from the road, then we'd creep through the strands of rusty barbed wire fence and skulk out into the field.

The grass was damp from the humidity and the summer rain, and it came up past our knees as we crouch-walked past the hulking cows, who stood in the heat like large boulders floating in a swollen sea of green. They watched us as we looked around for the mushrooms that wouldn't kill us if we ate them, but that would instead make us hallucinate.

After we had a couple of small bags filled with them, we'd sneak back to my truck, sometimes having to run from an angry farmer who would chase us with a shotgun until we were off his property, our arms and legs scratched by branches and thorns and barbed wire during our quick escape, which we always thought of as an adventure. One more exciting thing to do during the summer.

Then, I would drive while one of my friends sorted and counted the mushrooms we had picked, putting them on the cracked dashboard and rinsing them off with a bottle of water. After that we would eat them. But since the effects of the psilocybin weren't immediate, we had time to park my truck somewhere else, near a different set of woods, so we could walk and explore.

It was summer. July 4, 1996. The mosquitos buzzed around us, and the trees seemed to quiver with life; a slow vibration radiated outward from their leaves and branches like ripples of water emanating from where a stone had just broken through the water's silk surface of skin. Every sound was intensified. Colors melted into one another. Time slowed to a steady drip.

We walked through the woods that summer night, each experiencing our surroundings differently and distinctly, where everything was narrowed down to a bright pinprick of light and sound, then melted back into a singular Pangaea of matter, like molten steel. It felt as though we were walking through sheets of warm gauze, pools of thick, wet mud, and everything around us had become cloudy and blurred.

Eventually, we ended up on an old, abandoned train trestle that crossed over the Bogue Falaya River, which was a thin, brown string of water that looked black under the moonlight and whose darkness made the bright white shoals that flanked it look like bleached bones. We balanced over the crossties, the smell of creosote wafting upward as we went farther and farther down the tracks. The vines grew thicker, the bright green kudzu more and more dense, until it felt as though we were in a dark cave made of branches and leaves. My skin and hair were greasy, covered with sweat.

I bent down and placed my hand on the steel rail. Tried to feel for a vibration that might indicate an oncoming train. I knew the track was no longer in use, but I had seen the movie *Stand by Me* too many times to at least make me want to check. It was still surprisingly cool after baking in the summer sun all day. Crickets chirped somewhere off in the distance. My friends kept walking, and no one said anything to each other. We were each immersed in our own altered experience.

When we got to the other side of the trestle, we climbed down a rocky embankment that was littered with old newspapers and frayed clothes. A castoff tennis shoe. The remnants of an old trash fire. Half-broken bottles. A moldy sleeping bag. In the state I was in, I started to imagine that the lumps protruding from that old bag belonged to a person underneath. And I kept waiting for someone to rise up from the mound, wearing a torn shirt, stained and enshrouding their gaunt and dirty frame, sheaths of soggy newspaper fluttering down from them as they slowly stood to see who was intruding their space.

I pictured them like that: homeless and bedraggled by time and maybe guilt for something they'd done years before. Hungry. Just like the troll in "Three Billy Goats Gruff," waiting to devour us. That image persisted, became more vivid as my friends left me, making their way down the embankment and across the shoals toward the river. I could even imagine the whites of this person's otherwise bloodshot eyes—prominent and bright against their coal-dark, dirt-smeared face, the reek of cheap whiskey emanating from a toothless maw surrounded by a knotted, chest-length beard. All this as they croaked at me in a hardly used voice, "*Who's there?*"

It was like the voice my stepbrother and I had heard behind Saia's that night as we climbed into the cab of that forklift. Only then we had been much younger and were also sober, high only on the excitement of doing something wrong and not getting caught for it. So maybe it was my own guilt causing me to hear and imagine these things. After all, I was acting in ways I knew I shouldn't have been acting and doing things I knew I shouldn't have been doing.

I practically ran down that embankment then, trying to ignore the haunting image my mind had conjured as I caught up to my friends, who were all standing at the water's edge. We took off our shoes and shirts, rolled up our pants to our knees, and waded out into the middle of the river. The cool water rushed past us and lapped against our thighs. I looked up through a break in the trees overhead and could see the moon bathing in a black sea of diamond-colored stars. It was an almost-perfect white disk, with only just a small crescent of gray sliced out from its right side, yet steadily waning.

Still Life of an Old Library in Folsom, Louisiana

1.

See the old library there, a little one-room building at the end of a gravel lane, surrounded by tall grass and weeds and trees, a tiny cement bench out front for sitting and reading. The place is small, made up of white-flecked slats of clapboard siding and tar shingles, with big beds of brown pine needles on its roof. A small air-conditioning unit in one of the front windows chugs out cold air for the librarian working inside. It also keeps the books from getting damp and moldy, the pages warped and yellowed from all this humidity.

2.

The library is in the middle of a small, one-red-light town where the land rolls and sways into steep hills like the giant swells of an ocean, heaving. It is thick with pine woods in almost every direction, broken up in places by large blankets of pastureland that are pocked with horses and cows and smooth brown ponds for them to stand in and cool off if they want to. Sweet dusty hay is rolled up into bales as big as tractors, covered in clear plastic sheets of Visqueen or cracked blue tarps, and they edge the perimeters of the fields like boulders, while barns in various states of aging and decay blot out parts of the horizon like dark ink thumbprints on a sheet of crisp, clean paper. But still, it is beautiful here, and quiet. Peaceful. You can even see the stars in the sky at night, hear the crickets and the frogs and the buzz and hum of life out there, like you're living in a different time altogether.

3.

Back when I was a kid, the tiny village of Folsom, Louisiana, had a Baptist church, a post office, a diner, two hardware stores, a John's Curb Market where you could get Slush Puppies and candy cigarettes and rent VHS and Betamax tapes. There was a Jr. Food Mart where you could buy fried chicken and potato logs and cheeseburgers wrapped in tin foil from under a heat lamp. Another small grocery store called Bernie's had oil-darkened cement floors, and they sold Mary Jane's and IBC root beers in brown glass bottles that were cold and good. There was an elementary school and, of course, that tiny library where, when I was in first grade, our teacher would take us once a week to check out books.

We'd walk down the crooked spine of sidewalk, which was broken in places by large oak roots, rising up like arms digging their way out from under all that thick black loam. Then we'd go up Highway 25 until we got there, our whole class of twenty students.

4.

The library was about the size of a small storage shed, and I remember that only two or three of us could go in at a time. We would glance up at the dark shelves, the cracked spines of books limned only by a single sixty-watt light bulb that was suspended from a gray cord stapled to the rafters in the ceiling, or otherwise from a lonely slant of light coming in through one of the windows, and we would point to the book we wanted.

The librarian would reach up, get it down, open it, take a card out of it, mark the due date on the card with a rubber stamp, then slide the card back into the little pocket that was glued to the inside flap of the book, and hand it to us.

We would give her our library card, and she would record the entire transaction in her dusty ledger that sat open on the tall wooden desk in front of her. It was so high that you had to stand on your toes to even reach the edge of it.

5.

Most of the kids at my school didn't care about books, and they would make fun of me for reading them. But I did it anyway. I got books by Jules Verne, Mark Twain, S. E. Hinton, Franklin W. Dixon, Jack London, and Edgar Allan Poe. Even one by Stephen King when I was a little older, although the librarian still made me get permission first. I can remember the way all those books smelled, the way their pages felt, and, of course, the stories printed on them. It was all so magical to me. And it still is.

6.

I think I inherited my love for books from my biological mother and father, that it's in my genes. My mother had loved to read and tell stories ever since she was a child, and some of my first memories are of her reading to me in bed at night. My father, I learned—after I found out who he was when I was thirty-eight years old—is an avid reader as well: he has over nine hundred books listed on his online Goodreads account.

And then there's this: my mother's copy of *The Catcher in the Rye*, which I still have and which I read for the first time when I was about fourteen or fifteen years old. As an adult, I still like to open that book up sometimes, look at the title page on which my mother had written in dark blue ink her name and telephone number, then just beneath J. D. Salinger's name, in cursive, the words, "Good Book," which she underlined. Twice.

I also have her copy of *D'Aulaires' Book of Greek Myths* that her parents had given to her for Christmas one year. I used to love looking at all the drawings in there when I was a kid, then reading for hours the stories that went with them. Today, there's a slip of paper tucked between the front pages of that book from when my daughter used it to do a school project on Greek gods and goddesses not that long ago.

I only mention these things here to say something about the importance of books in my life. And to say this, too: that they saved me. Listen:

7.

I grew up in a single-wide trailer in the middle of about twenty acres of woods. We didn't have a car. We didn't have cable TV. It was before computers and internet, and even if those things had existed then, we probably wouldn't have been able to afford them, either. We were poor. The kind of poor that could change how a person thought about the world, and what their place was in it.

There was a lot of work to be done, too. We had horses, ducks, chickens, a large vegetable garden, peach trees that would make tons of those sweet, golden and mauve, fist-sized fruits every summer—which we then had to pick. I can still remember putting them in a scrap of quilt that we used to line the rust-covered wheelbarrow that we loaded them all into, as much as we could fit. But the thing is, we couldn't pick them fast enough and many of those peaches rotted on the grass as a result. And the other thing is, that could have easily been me. I could have been left there like that. To rot. But books got me out. Both reading them and then, eventually, writing them myself.

8.

When I was eleven years old, I took a faded, blue ledger book with lined paper inside, which my grandfather had given me to collect stamps in, and I carefully pulled the stamps out with a set of tweezers. Then, I used the blank pages to start writing a short story. It wasn't very good. It wasn't good at all actually, and so I never showed it to anyone. The point, though, is that I was writing.

And I would continue to: secretly making up stories and poems all through my adolescence and then into adulthood. I even tried to write a novel when I was sixteen after I found an old IBM Selectric typewriter in my grandparents' attic one day. I remember that it smelled thickly like the grease that had been used to oil the parts inside of it and that the keys were loud and heavy under my fingers. But it felt good to press on them.

I also remember the feeling of seeing words that I had written being printed one by one on a clean white sheet of paper as it spooled over the platen and then curled out and off onto the desk. I would stack the pages into a neat little pile. Doing this made me feel like a real writer, even back then: a professional who had let all of those stories he read as a kid engrave themselves onto his subconscious, like the glowing tip of a wood-burning tool pressed onto a piece of freshly cut pine. The seeds for my work had already been planted, and all I had to do was water them. So I did.

9.

Then, in what seemed like a rush of time and events, the thrum and pulse of years going by, I finally finished writing my first book. I was twenty-nine. Then, I wrote another one. And one more after that. I kept going. I didn't stop. In a way, those books became like all that fruit I had picked from those sagging peach trees as a kid. I just had to get as many of them in that wheelbarrow as I could before they had a chance to rot. Even now, I don't know if I would have been able to do all of that if I hadn't loved reading for so long, hadn't been able to check out all of those books from that librarian behind the tall desk.

10.

The library I went to as a kid has since moved into a more modern building on the other side of town. But the little shed where it once was is still there, still standing, though now it is vine-covered and chipped and mostly falling apart. You can still see the old address to the right of the door, though, the white metal numbers "13260" nailed to the wooden frame, where bright green vines have grown up to hide most of what else is left there: the slatted, wooden door and the rusty padlocked hasp that holds it shut; the roof that is covered now with thick tendrils of brown lichen and moss, where it all pulls up at the shingles, exposing the strips of black tar paper beneath.

One of the windows is sealed shut with a sheet of rain-darkened plywood, a green metal awning casting a rectangle of shadow over its surface, while several of the other ones are cracked in places and have broken panes of glass here and there. The air-conditioning unit is gone.

You can imagine families of raccoon or squirrels or rabbits or cute, little, brown field mice living inside, making nests in the rafters or on the sagging wooden shelves that once held all of those wonderful books. It's dark in there now, so you can't know for sure. But you can still glimpse the little, white curtains inside. Those are still there. You can even start to imagine the librarian putting them up one day—that would have been so long ago now, before you were even born—the sun coming in through the glass and warming her skin as she worked, stopping for just a second to brush off a skein of dust from the windowsill, so that everything would look nice and clean and new before all the children got there. One of them probably thinking already about all the books he would borrow and maybe even dreaming about all the ones he might someday write himself.

Truants

It was 1995. My friend Matt had just gotten his driver's license that past summer and his mom's old car, a gray Honda Civic with a hatchback and a stick shift in the center console. It had a tape deck, and he would drive to our house listening to Metallica and Megadeth and Pantera and AC/DC, the speakers in the door vibrating the tinted windows in their metal frames as he drove up our gravel driveway.

My stepmom didn't want my stepbrother and me riding in the car with anyone, but she had known Matt for years and he had spent many weekends at our trailer in Folsom, so sometimes she would let him pick us up on his way to school. There was something thrilling about riding to school in your friend's car like that, pulling up in the grass lot where the older kids parked their trucks and hung out, smoking cigarettes before class.

We were in tenth grade that year, and I hadn't gotten my own license yet. Usually, we'd ride the bus to school, or my stepmom would take us if we woke up late. In fact, she had dropped us off that morning when we decided, just after second period, to skip the rest of the day.

My stepbrother and Matt and I all met in the commons area next to one of the Coke machines and told a couple of our friends we were leaving, probably just to see what their reaction would be, but more likely to elevate our status to that of people who actually did things like skip school in the first place. We didn't have anywhere to go, anything really to do, but it felt important that we were leaving that morning.

After the bell rang and a few students were still left in the hallways, running toward their classrooms so they wouldn't be marked tardy, Matt and my stepbrother and I walked out the side entrance and to the parking lot. We moved quickly, but also as though we were supposed to be doing that, trying to avoid suspicion by seeming confident and in control, like we knew where we were going and why we were going there.

No one saw us as we climbed into the little car. Matt turned on the radio and rolled down the windows. We pulled out of the school and headed down West 21st Avenue toward Covington.

"What do y'all wanna do?" Matt asked, yelling over the wind rush and the music. My stepbrother was riding upfront and I was sitting in the cramped seat in the back, so I had to lean up for them to hear me.

"Jenn skipped school today, too," I said. "We could always go to her house and see what she's up to."

Jenn was a girl whom I was somewhat dating, though we hadn't actually gone on any dates. I was really more infatuated with her than anything else, and I think she probably just liked me out of boredom. She had come over to my trailer in Folsom a couple of times when my stepparents weren't home, staying at my neighbor Stacey's house, and then they'd both sneak through the woods when it was dark so we could hang out.

But I was so young and nervous I didn't know what to do once she was there. We would sit on the sofa and make out for a while, and when she got up and pulled me into my bedroom, easing into my tiny bunkbed and then reaching up for me to get on top of her, I would think of a reason to leave the room or otherwise just climb in next to her and keep making out. I could never go any further than that.

Jenn wasn't older than me, just more experienced, and I was intimidated by her. Once she had sat on the trampoline in my backyard and asked me to bite her neck. Stacey was there with us, and Jenn had asked her to bite her neck, too. So, we both sat there with Jenn between us as we bit her flesh and she sighed with what I guess was some kind of pleasure. At fifteen, everything feels so confusing and weird, it's hard to say what is going on at any given time. I was simply overwhelmed by my feelings for Jenn, and I didn't want her to think I wasn't attracted to her, but I also didn't want her to think I was scared—which I was.

Even though she had tried to get me to sleep with her, and even though God knows I wanted to, I was afraid—not of disease or pregnancy or any of the things they warn you against in school. I had no moral objections to it. I was a fifteen-year-old boy. All I thought about was sex. But when it came down to it, I was terrified. Scared I wouldn't know what to do, how to do it. That I would be no good at it and would thus be humiliated.

I remember one time being at my grandmother's house of all places, sitting on the sofa next to Jenn underneath a blanket while we feigned watching a movie on TV. Stacey was there too, sitting on the other side of Jenn as Jenn reached her hand over to my leg and started rubbing my jeans. I was immediately turned on, and I knew Jenn could tell. She moved her fingers over me slowly, feeling me with her palm lightly brushing over my jeans, but never taking her eyes from the movie on TV. I tried to lean back into the sofa, to let myself ease into what was happening without anyone noticing.

Jenn moved her fingers up and down, slowly, but she kept her hand on the outside of my jeans. The movie kept playing, and Stacey pretended not to notice what was going on. I was sweating now. My stomach felt tight, clenched in on itself. Something was on the verge of happening. And then Jenn just stopped. She looked at me for a moment before turning back to the movie. And that was it. I knew what it could be like with her, but I wouldn't know for sure, she seemed to be saying, unless I made the next move. But I never did.

And now here I was, trying to convince Matt to drive to her house.

Matt said, "Man, I don't wanna go over there. I can't *stand* her."

"What do you care?" I said. "We don't have anything better to do."

"Shit, dude," he said. "I guess we can pick her up. I don't know, but I don't want to hang out at her house all day."

"Yeah, that's fine, man. I doubt she'll want to either," I said. I had thought maybe Matt could drop me off over there, and Jenn and I could be alone. Her mom was at work and who knew what could have happened? But I also knew it would be a betrayal to Matt and my stepbrother to ditch them like that. Besides, they could have just left me there, and I'd be stuck. It wasn't worth the risk.

When we got to her house, Jenn was sitting outside on the front porch smoking a cigarette; it was as if she had known we were coming. I watched her as she stood up and walked out to the driveway, where we were waiting in Matt's car.

"Hey," she said. "What are y'all doing here?"

"I don't know," I said. "Just driving around, I guess."

Jenn dropped the cigarette on the gravel driveway and rubbed it out with her tennis shoe. Then she bent down and picked it up and stuffed it in the pack. She put it in her back pocket, making a square against her tight jeans. I looked away but could still see the reflection of her long legs in the car's sideview mirror. I was hoping she'd come with us, wherever it was we were headed.

"Do you wanna come with us?" I said.

"Yeah," she said. "That'd be cool. Just let me go get my purse real quick."

"Okay. Cool."

I could sense Matt tensing up; he had probably been hoping she wouldn't come. Then, I watched Jenn through the sideview mirror as she walked back up the driveway and then onto the screened-in porch. A little dog barked from inside the house.

"Shit," Matt was saying now, more to my stepbrother than to me. "I wish she wasn't coming."

My stepbrother didn't say anything, just sat there looking out the window. I don't think he liked Jenn either.

Anyway, Jenn got in the small car and Matt had to lift his seat forward and nearly press his cheek to the steering wheel so she could climb in to where I was sitting. Once she was in, Matt put his seat back, closed the door, then slipped Ozzy Osbourne's *Bark at the Moon* into the cassette player and turned it up loud. He had two big speakers stuffed into the trunk, just under the hatchback window behind Jenn and me. I could feel the bass vibrating against my neck and back and shoulders.

Then he pulled out of the driveway and turned onto Tyler Street, heading toward downtown Covington.

"Can you please turn that down?" Jenn said, tapping Matt on the shoulder.

"What?"

"Can you turn it down?" she said again.

Matt didn't answer her, just dialed the knob a bit to the left so the music wasn't as loud. I could see him through the rearview mirror rolling his eyes. Then, Jenn scooted closer to me. Nobody said anything.

We kept driving.

Finally, my stepbrother said something about the new Super Wal-Mart that had just opened. Until recently the only Wal-Mart was down the road, closer to the interstate, and it was a pretty small store as far as Wal-Marts go. You couldn't get groceries there or anything like that.

But this new Wal-Mart was supposed to be gigantic, and none of us had been to it yet.

"Y'all wanna go?" Matt said, looking at Jenn and me through the rearview mirror.

I looked at Jenn, who just shrugged. "Yeah," I said. "That's cool with me."

So, we drove up Highway 190 and turned in to the sprawling asphalt parking lot, climbed out the car, and walked inside. The whole time I kept looking around to make sure we didn't see anyone we knew. I kept feeling on edge since we were supposed to be in school. I didn't know if cops could bust you for that or not, but I didn't want to take any chances.

I was also worried that Jenn might try to take something from the store without paying for it. She often bragged about the clothes and tapes and movies and makeup she would steal from the mall in Slidell when she went there with her other friends. It was just something else to do out of boredom, I guess, but I didn't want to get in that kind of trouble if I could avoid it.

Matt and my stepbrother went to look at the tapes in the music section, and Jenn and I walked around somewhat aimlessly. I remember being amazed that there was a McDonald's in the back of the store. An actual place where you could sit down and eat food. I had never seen anything like it. It seemed phenomenal at the time.

After a while, though, we got bored, and I could tell Jenn was starting to get restless. Fidgety. She kept sighing and rolling her eyes, looking pouty. Then she said she wanted to go back home before her mom got there; and, anyway, we needed to start driving to Folsom to meet my own stepmom at the bus stop. Our plan was to tell her that we missed the bus, and that Matt just gave us a ride home. We were feeling pretty good about the whole idea, like we actually might pull it off.

But after we dropped Jenn off at her house, then drove up Highway 25 back to Folsom and got to the bus stop, my stepmom's car wasn't there like it should've been. I knew the bus hadn't come yet so maybe she was running late, I thought.

"I guess we can just wait," I told Matt. "She'll probably be here in a minute."

"Yeah," he said, then just turned the radio back up and looked out the window. He still seemed irritated with me for having to hang around Jenn all day.

A minute passed. Then ten. Then twenty. We had already watched our bus come and go, depositing its load of kids to walk the rest of the way home or otherwise get in the car with their parents, like we were supposed to have done, but our stepmom just wasn't there.

After a while, we decided to drive back to our trailer to see if anyone was home, thinking that maybe some line of communication had gotten crossed earlier. I was starting to feel nervous, though. And this feeling was only intensified when we pulled up the long gravel driveway and saw that my stepmom's car wasn't parked where it was supposed to be. In fact, no one appeared to be home at all.

"Shit, man," Matt said. "Where is she?"

"I don't know," my stepbrother said.

"Let's go back to the bus stop again," I said. "Maybe she's there and we just missed her or something."

"Yeah," Matt said. None of us knew what else to do.

So, we drove back to the bus stop, and this time we saw my stepmom's car right away. She was already rolling down her window and staring at us. She didn't look happy.

"Hey, Ms. Gretchen," Matt said as he pulled up alongside the idling car, smiling, trying to play everything off as best he could.

"Get y'all's asses back home," my stepmom said.

"What?" my stepbrother asked, looking over Matt and through the rolled-down window.

"You heard me, son. Get your asses home. Now."

I sort of slouched down in the back seat, not saying anything. There was nothing to say. Somehow it seemed she had figured out what we had done.

Then she pulled away and turned onto Highway 25, heading north toward our trailer, driving fast. Matt followed her.

"Man, we're fucked," I said. "She looked pissed. I wonder how she found out."

"I don't know," Matt said. "But y'all are gonna be in some shit now, dude."

We pulled up in the driveway behind my stepmom's van, which was still running. I could see her sitting inside still. Then, we got out of Matt's car and started walking toward the porch. My stepmom got out and followed us and just as we got to the first step going up, she slapped Matt across his cheek. Not hard but enough to scare us. She never hit my stepbrother or me and now she was hitting our friend.

"Where in the hell were y'all?" she said.

"What?" my stepbrother said.

"Don't 'what' me, Bryan. I went to y'all's school and y'all weren't there. You made me look like a complete moron."

"We got a ride home with Matt," I said, still trying to hold on to the lie of the original story we had planned to tell. "We missed the bus."

"David, don't lie to me. Y'all didn't even stay at school today. I went to check y'all out because your grandfather had a heart attack this morning."

"God, which one?" I said.

"Your stepdad's dad."

"Is he okay?"

"They don't know. He's in the hospital. All I know is that I get to y'all's school this morning and the lady at the desk calls your classrooms, and y'all aren't there. 'Sure they're here,' I told her. 'I just dropped them off a little while ago.'

"'Well, ma'am, they're not in class. I don't know what to tell you. Maybe they skipped?'

"'*Skipped*?' I told her. 'My sons don't skip school.' The lady just laughed at me. Do you know how embarrassing that was?"

"Sorry, Ms. Gretchen," Matt said.

"Just get your ass home, Matt. I don't want to hear anything from you right now at all."

"Yes, ma'am," Matt said, looking down at his shoes. His cheek was still red from where my stepmom had slapped him. You could see the marks from her fingers on his face. "Later, y'all," he said to me and my stepbrother.

"Later," we said.

Then we watched him as he walked back to his car and drove away. My stepmom's van was still running, and my younger stepsister was sitting in her car seat in the back.

"Y'all don't have time to go inside," my stepmom was saying now. "Everyone's still waiting at the hospital."

"Is he okay?" Bryan said.

"I told y'all I don't know, son."

"Is Dad there?" he said.

"Of course he is."

"Does he know we skipped school?" I said.

"Yeah, David, he knows. I had to call him to tell him why we couldn't be at the hospital until later. That y'all's asses weren't where you were supposed to be when I came to get you."

I didn't say anything. There was nothing else to say. And so, the hour-long drive to the hospital was quiet and tense. Plenty of time to reflect on what we had done and where we were going and what might be about to happen.

*

My grandfather managed to hang on for a little while after that, and my stepdad was too distracted to say anything to us about skipping school. It felt horrible, though. It probably would have been better to just get in trouble instead of quietly feeling selfish and immature and irresponsible like that. And to know that everyone in our family knew it, too.

But no one else said anything about us skipping, and we eventually decided to leave when the doctors said there was not much more they could do. My stepdad stayed though, and when he came back home later that evening and I asked him how our grandfather was doing, all he said as he stood in the doorway was, "He's gone, babe."

Then he looked away, still holding the screen door open with his arm, but I could tell he was sobbing. His eyes were red, and his mouth quivered slightly. It was the first time I had ever seen my stepfather cry like that. And it didn't seem to matter anymore that my stepbrother and I had skipped school that day, had gotten caught, and had embarrassed our family.

This was something important, and I still remember how my stepdad put his head in his hands that night. The sound of his crying, how it echoed and bled through the thin walls of our trailer. Like something that was trying to get away, to escape from the place where it had been trapped for too long. Even if leaving meant it could never come back. Or if it did, nothing would ever be the same again anyway.

Drivers' Ed

I t's Saturday. Early in the morning and my stepparents are already dropping me off at a strip mall in downtown Covington, Louisiana, where I'm going to spend the next eight hours taking a drivers' education course so that I can get my license the following week. I'm only fifteen, but back then you could do that. No semester-long classes during high school. No learner's permit. Back then, you could just get your license after a one-day class.

We never did much on Saturdays anyway. My stepdad just sat on the sofa and watched Clint Eastwood movies all day, the images flickering across the grainy screen of the little TV that rested on top of the bigger, broken set in the den. We only got about three or four channels on a clear day and there was always a wad of aluminum foil wrapped around the antennas to—hopefully—help them catch a decent signal.

On Saturdays and Sundays, those channels showed lots of old action and western movies. Things with Charles Bronson, Chuck Norris, John Wayne. I'm not sure if my stepdad really even liked those movies that much, or if it was just a matter of there not being anything else to watch.

Sometimes we'd rent a VCR and he'd put on the four-part, six-and-a-half hour long, western epic, *Lonesome Dove*, based on the Larry McMurtry novel. It would consume his entire day, him sitting on the sofa with his pack of crumpled Marlboros and his glass of Budweiser sweating on the coffee table, which was made from the hatch door of an old shrimp boat, I remember.

And that's what he did on the weekends—sit on the sofa watching movies. When I was a teenager and my friends started to come over sometimes, they called him "the rooster." I never knew why until I was listening to that Alice in Chains song one time, the one about the Vietnam veteran who comes back home with PTSD, and then I knew why they called him that.

And even though my stepdad hadn't been to Vietnam, I could see why my friends thought he was crazy. He looked a lot like Jack Nicholson did in *The Shining*, except with a full beard. He was shorter than I was, but good-looking and very strong. He had been a boxer when he was younger, and you could tell by the way he was built.

But most weekends, while my stepdad sat on the sofa watching movies, my stepmom and stepbrother and I cut the grass outside with a Weed eater (our lawnmower had quit working years before and we'd never had the money to get it fixed). And all of this is just to say that spending the day in a driving class was preferable to almost anything else I could have been doing. A couple of times, I even got a Saturday detention on purpose when I was in junior high just to get out of the house, like Ally Sheedy did in *The Breakfast Club*.

Anyway, today it's cool outside, and overcast, the gray clouds hanging low and spraying a damp mist on the otherwise empty parking lot. So, I get out of my stepparents' car and walk toward the building, and then I hear them pull out and drive away.

I see a couple of other kids about my age milling around just inside the door, a few of them at a desk shuffling papers, and so I walk in.

The room is spare, like an office building—Berber carpet and gray-white walls with nothing on them save for a few of those inspirational posters that you can buy at Office Depot: a lion overlooking a vast savanna with the word PRIDE emblazoned in golden letters beneath his strong, swishing tail; a formation of jets cutting across a perfectly clear blue sky, the word TEAMWORK riding under the trails of white clouds being emitted from their wings.

There's a conference table stretching the distance of the narrow room, a TV/VCR cart at the head of the table where a video is already set up, but paused on the tiny screen, the little lines of static sizzling across the frozen image like arteries. I walk to the end of the room and sit down in one of the plastic chairs. Then, I wait while the instructor shuffles some papers into a clipboard. He finally approaches the front of the room.

"I'm Gregg," he says, his smile revealing a mouth full of perfectly white teeth. "How many of you guys are ready to *drive*!" It's more of an exclamation the way he says it, less of a question, which might be why no one really says anything in response.

"Okay," he says, a little less excitedly, maybe even a little defeated by our lack of enthusiasm. "Let's get started then."

We spend the morning watching videos about driving safety, seat belt use, hazardous weather conditions, road signs. Occasionally, Gregg pauses the video so we can take a quiz, review information we'd just seen. Yet Gregg's mood seems to darken as the day wears on. I'll never know why. Maybe it's the overcast sky outside, but his energy level seems to be slowly draining, like soapy, gray dishwater in a sink. He starts to look like most of the teachers I've had and have troubled with my presence over the years.

For some reason, seeing Gregg's diminishing state reminds me of when I was in the eighth grade at Folsom Junior High School and had cheated on a science test. I had never done anything like that before and I can still remember the teacher, Mr. Core, who also taught agriculture, shop, 4-H, and P. E. The school itself was small, with only about four to five hundred students at most, and the teachers often taught several subjects like that.

Mr. Core's classroom was attached to the side of the gym, I remember—it was a square, brick building with high windows and a large closet at the front where he kept P. E. supplies, shop tools, and large plastic buckets of beef jerky, which he sold for fifty cents a stick at the beginning of every class. And test days were no different. At least ten minutes of the early part of class were spent on these transactions.

I was in my desk, looking over my notes one last time before the test, nervous because I hadn't studied the night before. When I finally looked up from my notes, I saw that about half the class was still lined up at Mr. Core's desk, buying sticks of beef jerky while the rest of the students sat at their desks, flipping through their notes and textbooks. I could also see the boy in front of me, Jeremiah Fussell, writing notes on the palm of his hand.

I tapped him on the shoulder to let him know I could see what he was doing and that possibly Mr. Core could as well. Jeremiah just smiled and assured me he wouldn't get caught. He always did this, he said. On every test.

I looked back up at Mr. Core, who still seemed busy and distracted counting money and passing out sticks of beef jerky. He hadn't once glanced up from what he was doing. And Jeremiah's words, "I never get caught," kept echoing in my head. I noticed two or three other kids around me. They were doing the same thing. I wondered if Mr. Core knew about this and just allowed it. Like it was an unspoken ritual in his class I hadn't known about until then.

So, I started writing on my own hand. I wrote words like *photosynthesis, nucleus, atomic particle*. No definitions. Just the words. I hadn't thought about how this would actually help me on the test. I just wrote and wrote without thinking until my palm and wrist were tattooed with words from my notebook.

When Mr. Core finally put the plastic lids back onto the jars of beef jerky and all the other students had begun to sit down again, closing their books and sliding them under their desks, Mr. Core started passing out the tests. He set mine down and I wrote my name on the top of the page. Then the date. Then I started answering some of the questions, most of whose answers came to me right away, without the aid of the words I had written on my hand and wrist. I almost forgot I had written them there at all until I looked up and saw Mr. Core coming down the aisle and raising the free hands of some of the kids on my row.

He didn't say anything, but when he saw writing on anyone's palm, he just picked up their test and drew a big red zero across it. The students sat there as if in shock. I looked down at my test and kept writing answers—and they were the right ones, I knew that—hoping he wouldn't come to me, that he'd know I would never do anything like cheat on a test, that I was a good student, for the most part.

But he kept coming down the aisle, lifting hands.

Then he stopped right beside my desk, picked up my left arm by the wrist, looked at my hand, then at me. I glanced down at my desk but could still see him shaking his head slowly from left to right as he drew a large red zero across the top of my paper.

"I'm disappointed in you, Armand," he said. Then he kept walking down the aisle toward the back of the classroom, lifting wrists and checking hands one after the other.

And now, sitting in drivers' ed a couple of years later, I still have that same sense of failure, of letting someone down, taking up someone's Saturday so he can try to teach a group of kids something they really couldn't care less about. It's a feeling that never leaves me. I wonder why I'm here.

*

When it's time for lunch, I walk a couple of blocks to hang out with this girl I know from school. We'd been friends for a couple of years, and since she lives close by, I figure I can drop in and we can eat lunch or something together. Her name's Tiffany.

"What are you doing here?" she asks when she opens the door after I knock on it a few times.

Then, I tell her about drivers' ed, and she just says, "Oh." She asks me if I want to come in.

"Sure," I say. The sky is still worked up into a steady drizzle and I don't have an umbrella or anything, so my hair and shirt and clothes are fairly damp.

Tiffany hands me a towel as we walk inside, and I follow her to the kitchen as I dry off my hair and clothes. After that, we sit down and eat some Fritos and talk a little.

"Where's your mom?" I ask her.

"At work."

"Cool."

"Hey, I have an idea," she says suddenly. "You want to do some shots?"

"What?"

"Whiskey? Vodka? I don't know. I have some of those little bottles like they used to give people on airplanes."

"Sure," I say. "Why not?"

"Cool. My mom keeps a bunch of 'em in the cabinet up there. She won't ever know they're gone. She has like fifty of them."

I watch Tiffany get up, pull the chair she's been sitting on across the linoleum and toward the counter, where she stands up and reaches into one of the cabinets. She brings down a half dozen tiny bottles—three Evan Williams with the green label on them and three bottles of Taaka vodka. She comes over to the table, puts her chair back, and sits down.

We drink a few bottles each. I have the bourbon, she has the vodka, and with our empty stomachs, we get drunk fast. A couple of times she rubs on my calf with her foot. She's wearing socks and no shoes. But I'm starting to get nervous about getting back to class on time, hoping I'm not too drunk. I pull my leg back and stick it between the wooden rungs of my chair.

"I probably should get back," I say.

"Yeah," she says. "I guess I'll see you in school on Monday?"

"Probably."

When I stand up, the booze really starts to hit me. My head spins a little bit, and my skin feels kind of tingly and weird, probably because I haven't eaten anything all day except for those Fritos. Tiffany doesn't have any food to offer me. She doesn't have any gum or any mints either. I just hope the driving instructor Gregg won't smell the alcohol on my breath. I walk back to class through the rain, feeling buzzed, the leaves on the trees and the grass glistening in the misty air.

I'm a little late getting back.

"So kind of you to join us, Mr. Armand," Gregg says. Everyone laughs. "You're fifteen minutes late," he says.

"Sorry," I say, "I kind of lost track of time."

Gregg doesn't say anything, just clicks his white teeth with his tongue and rolls his eyes, then points to the empty seat where I had been sitting earlier. I can feel him watching me as I walk over to it and sit. I slouch down as low as I can.

The rest of the afternoon is somewhat of a blur. The girl sitting next to me—her name is Fallon—finally whispers into my ear. "Jesus, man, you're *drunk*. I can freakin' *smell* the booze on you. Where'd you even *go*?"

"Nowhere," I say. "I just went to get a hamburger." My head starts to throb a little bit. "And I'm not *drunk*," I say.

"Yeah, right," she says.

We spend the rest of the afternoon filling out paperwork and then taking the final test that will determine if we receive credit for this course, thus enabling us to get our licenses from the DMV the following week. I'm trying very hard to concentrate, to make sure I get as many answers right as I can. But my head is spinning, my skin is still tingling, and I keep wanting to laugh at the pictures on the test: the friendly police officers, the smiling crossing guards. All these happy families driving together, the wind blowing their hair, their eyes covered with dark sunglasses as they head to beaches or amusement parks.

When I am about three-quarters done, I see my stepparents pull up outside. Gregg looks out of the window from where he is sitting at his desk, reading a copy of *News on Wheels*. I can see their headlights through the rain, the windshield wipers sluicing water back and forth across the glass.

"I'll be right back," Gregg says. "Everyone, keep your eyes on your own tests." Then, he looks at his wristwatch and walks out the door. The little bell at its corner jingles brightly.

Fallon looks at me, whispers, "Isn't that your stepparents?"

"Yeah," I say, trying to keep my eyes on my test so the room won't start spinning.

"Why are they so early?" Fallon says. "It's only like three o'clock."

"I don't know," I say. And I really don't have any idea.

A minute or two later, Gregg comes back inside grinning and shaking his head. But he does not look happy. Or amused.

"Y'all," he says, interrupting our test. Everyone looks up.

"Everything you've been told today about what *not* to do behind the wheel of a car, those people outside are doing. If I didn't know better, I'd think this was some kind of joke. Like on *Candid Camera*."

Fallon suddenly says, and loud enough so that the whole class can hear this time, "David, aren't those your stepparents?"

I don't say anything. I try to pretend I'm still concentrating on my test, that I haven't noticed my stepparents outside, but Fallon says it again.

"David," she says. "Look. Those are *your* stepparents in that car he's talking about, isn't it?"

Now everyone in the classroom is looking out the window. Gregg is also looking, as if maybe he had imagined the whole thing, but occasionally he turns and stares back at me, as though he's trying to make a connection between two electrical circuits that have been split apart.

"Mr. Armand," he says. "Can you come up here for a second?"

I stand, a bit wobbly still, and start walking toward his desk. I just hope he can't smell the booze on my breath.

As I hover in front of Gregg, I see the paperwork he's been filling out all afternoon, the red checks and Xs next to our names. I have no idea what these could indicate but it reminds me again of Mr. Core and that red zero he had drawn across my science test that time. I don't have a chance to see what mark Gregg put next to my name before he finally says, "So, those are your stepparents out there?"

"Yeah."

"Okay. I want you to do me a favor then. I want you to go out there and tell them that I work for the sheriff's office and that I can have both of them arrested right now."

"Why?" I say. "What are they doing?"

"Well, for one," he says, looking up at the class and noticing that we're being watched, then tuning his voice down to a whisper, "neither one of them is wearing a seatbelt, there's an open can of beer in the console, and your stepmom is holding a child *in her lap*." He emphasizes these last words as though it is the most unheard-of concept one can imagine.

"Oh, that's my stepsister," I say. "She usually rides in her car seat. My stepmom probably just took her out since they're parked right there. She was probably just crying or something."

"Well, either way, just go out there and tell them what I told you."

"Okay."

I start toward the door, just wanting this to all be over. Then, Gregg says, "And I'm not really a cop. Just tell them that anyway, though. See what they say."

As I walk outside into the rain, I can hear the rest of the class whispering and laughing quietly. The little overhead bell chirps again and I try to think of how I can explain this to my stepparents. My stepdad has a very bad temper, especially when he's been drinking, and I know he won't hesitate to cause a scene. I know that he would probably *enjoy* kicking the shit out of someone like Gregg. I just can't give him an excuse to do so. Plus, I can't let him know that I've been drinking myself.

As I very slowly make my way out to their car, I think about the first time I got drunk. I was only eleven years old. I was in the sixth grade, and we were at a Christmas party at my stepdad's brother's house in Chalmette. My stepbrother and I were both at the age where we didn't believe in Santa Claus anymore, which took a good bit of the magic out of the holiday, and so we didn't really want to play with the other kids who were there; they were mostly younger cousins and distant relatives, anyway.

So, we were sitting at the bar just off the side of the kitchen, drinking Sprite from little plastic Dixie cups and eating peanuts mixed with M&Ms from a glass bowl. My stepdad's brother was standing behind the bar, serving drinks, and he was pretty drunk himself. He had two daughters, but said he'd always wanted boys—kids he could toughen up and straighten out. He'd been a marine.

I remember him looking around the room to see if anyone was watching him, then pulling two tiny little bottles (what everyone I knew back then called "ponies") of Miller High Life from an ice chest at his feet and then setting them on the bar in front of my stepbrother and me.

"Y'all drink these," he said. "It'll put hair on your chest."

His face and cheeks were red (much like my stepdad's would get when he drank too much), and he was smiling and talking a lot. Usually, he was pretty quiet, a heavy silence hanging over him that made me feel intimidated and scared—more so, even, than I was of my own stepdad. People called my stepdad's brother a hard-ass, and I was more terrified to disobey him than I was of what my stepdad would do if he saw me drinking. My stepdad was younger than his brother, and it seemed like that man was the only person who my stepdad was intimidated by.

So, I picked up the little bottle and sipped from it. It tasted horrible. I looked over at my stepbrother, who was sipping from his bottle as well, and then at my stepdad's older brother, who was watching both of us.

"Come on, boys," he said. "Don't be little pussies. Drink up."

I took another sip, then another. My stepbrother, I could see, was doing the same with his.

When the bottles were empty, my stepdad's brother handed us each another one. And we kept drinking.

At some point, I remember, my stepdad walked past, and instead of being enraged to see these two eleven-year-old boys chugging away like that, he just patted us each on the back. It was as if we were completing a rite of passage or something, and five or six beers later, our own faces reddened from the alcohol coursing through our blood, someone took a picture of us sitting there at the bar. Drunk and smiling. My stepmom kept that picture framed on her nightstand for years.

When I finally get to the car, the rain has slackened to a warm and steady mist, but the sky is still gray and overcast. I walk to the passenger side of the car where my stepmom is sitting, and indeed, as Gregg had said, she's holding my stepsister in her lap. My stepmom rolls down the window.

"Almost finished?" she says, as though nothing at all is out of the ordinary.

"Yeah," I say. "Almost. He just has to grade our tests and stuff."

My stepdad is sitting there behind the wheel, the engine idling, a cold can of Budweiser between his legs, darkening his jeans where the condensation is building up on his thighs.

"That guy that just came out here is your teacher?" he says.

"Yeah."

"When you go back in there, do me a favor and tell him I said he's an asshole."

"*Clint*," my stepmom says to him, as if talking to a child.

I laugh a little bit, still trying to think of a way to avoid provoking my stepdad's temper by telling him what Gregg had said about him.

"I should go in there and beat his fucking ass," my stepdad says. He takes a gulp from his beer. At least that will keep him from smelling the booze on me, I think.

"Why?" I say. "What'd he tell y'all?"

"Nothing," my stepdad says. "He's just a little prick."

I don't know what to say, so I just stand there in the rain. I look back toward the building and can see our reflections in the tinted windows. I imagine everyone in the class staring out at us and laughing but I can't see anyone inside.

"Well, just get your ass back in there and finish your test," my stepdad says. His cheeks are beer-reddened, and he looks angry and drunk. Way more drunk than I am. Though no one seems to notice that, thankfully.

"Okay," I say. "But that guy wanted me to come out here and tell you that he was with the sheriff's office. He said that y'all shouldn't be riding around without seatbelts and that open beer can."

"What?" my stepdad says. Now his hand is on the door handle as if he's about to get out of the car. My stepmom touches her fingers against his arm.

"Clint. Wait," she says. Then, she looks at me. "Why'd he tell you all that, David?"

"I don't know," I say. "Just don't do anything. *Please.* I'll be finished in there in a minute."

"That little motherfucker," my stepdad says, looking out through the wet windshield and at the door behind which Gregg is likely standing, looking back at us. But my stepdad doesn't get out of the car, and Gregg doesn't come back out into the rain.

Which is good.

Because my stepdad's temper can be vile.

He had once kicked out the back window in a police cruiser after getting arrested for disturbing the peace. He kept a sawed-off shotgun under his seat everywhere he went. It's probably sitting there right now, I think, peeking out against the floorboard.

I think about the time I was in the car with him when he was arrested a few years earlier, how he'd managed to control his temper for once. I remember it well, how we were driving home one morning after hunting on my grandfather's property out in Folsom, the back of my stepdad's little Mazda pickup truck loaded with quail, our shotguns (my stepbrother and I had .410s, my stepdad and grandfather each had a twelve gauge), and an ice chest, when I heard my stepdad say, "Shit."

He was looking in the rearview mirror, and when I turned to see what he was looking at, I saw a police cruiser behind us, its blue lights flashing. He pulled over.

My grandfather was riding with us, my stepbrother and I squeezed in the small cab between them, and we all just waited as the officer approached the truck. Then, my stepdad rolled down his window.

"Can I see your license and registration, please?" the officer said.

"Ed," my stepdad said, looking over at my grandfather now. "Hand me the registration out the glove compartment, will you?"

My grandfather did this, handing the folded paper over to my stepdad. He didn't say anything. My stepdad passed it to the officer.

"Your license?" the officer said, still appearing to examine the registration card.

"I don't have it," my stepdad said.

The officer looked up from the paperwork, paused, then said, "I'm going to have to ask you to step out of the car, sir." I watched as my stepdad climbed out of the cab and another police cruiser passed us, then pulled on to the shoulder in front of where we were parked. I could hear the gravel crunching under the tires as the car stopped and another officer emerged.

The next thing I saw was both officers pressing my stepdad against the side of their car and placing him in handcuffs. I remember seeing him look up at me and his face and the way it looked through the cracked windshield. I didn't know what was happening then or why.

Then, one of the cops came back over to the truck and looked through the window at us.

"Can you get these two boys home?" he said to my grandfather.

"Yes, sir," he said. "I will."

"Well, just so you know, I'm arresting Mr. Armand here because a complaint came in from the horse farm just up the road from where y'all were hunting. They said that they could hear, like, pellets hitting their roof from where y'all was shootin' them guns back there. Enough to scare the hell out of all them poor horses. But them folks had the good sense to write down your license plate number as y'all was leavin', gave a good description of this here truck."

"I own that property," my grandfather said. "We weren't doing anything illegal."

"I wouldn't say that," the officer said. "When we went out there to respond to the call, we seen where y'all had seeded that land. That's illegal. It's also illegal that these boys ain't wearin seat belts. I can let that go, but Mr. Armand over there is driving without a license. Not to mention he's been drinkin'. That ice chest back there's full of beer. And I'm willing to bet y'all ain't got huntin' licenses neither."

The officer stopped talking, maybe to let that last part hold some more weight.

Then he said, "Y'all get on home now. And you have a good day."

My grandfather didn't say anything, just climbed out of the truck and walked around to the driver's side, where he got into the cab and started the engine. Then he put it in gear and pulled back out onto the road. As we passed the police cruiser, I glanced over and saw my stepdad sitting in the back seat, looking out at us. Then he was gone.

But he's here now, and I don't want to anger him, so I just go inside, finish my test, then watch Gregg as he marks it up. I breathe carefully through my nose, hoping he can't smell the alcohol on me.

"Well," he finally says. "Congratulations, Mr. Armand. You passed."

He starts to fill out another form, then looks up at me. "So, what did your folks say? About me being a cop?"

"Nothing," I say. "My stepmom's going to drive us home, put my stepsister back in her car seat."

"Good," Gregg says, looking proud of himself for what he'd said earlier. Then, he hands me the certificate that says I passed the course. "And I sure do hope you never pick up any of their bad habits," he says.

"I won't," I say, my head still spinning from the booze, knowing that it's probably already too late. I want to tell Gregg that I've been seeing this sort of thing my whole life, that drinking seems so normal to me that I just assume everyone does it.

I want to tell him that my grandmother used to keep a wooden plaque in her kitchen that said, "Never Trust A Man That Doesn't Drink." And I grew up believing that, seeing my grandmother pop open a can of Budweiser at eleven o'clock every morning, sometimes even as early as ten. I remember the bottles of Evan Williams sitting on the kitchen counter and how every day at around five o'clock—sometimes four—she'd unscrew the cap and fix herself a highball.

I remember visiting her in rehab when I was nine years old and playing horseshoes with my stepbrother as my stepparents talked to her on the covered patio, how angry she was for having to be there. And how she started drinking again almost as soon as she got out.

I want to listen to Gregg, to not adopt those bad habits, and to not cheat at it either, like I did on that science test—the disappointment I caused. I really want to do the right thing. But how will I do that? I wonder. All I know is that I want to be better than I am.

"Thanks," I say, but I can't tell if he hears me. I stumble a little bit through the door and outside, still drunk, into the rain, where my stepparents are waiting for me so that we can all just drive back home.

Real Work

When I was fifteen or sixteen, I moved out of my abusive home and away from my alcoholic stepdad for several weeks, during which time I lived with friends, hitchhiking rides from school to various places where I was staying or to various jobs where I was working.

I remember washing dishes for a few nights at a pizza place in Covington, Louisiana. One of my friends from high school had helped me get that job. It was a small, dingy little restaurant and there weren't any waiters or people to bus tables, so I had to do that, too. Then I'd go back into the greasy kitchen and wash all the dirty things I had collected from the booths.

On my first night there, the manager, Ms. Cindy, showed me how to punch my time card and where to hang my apron (it was a used one with someone else's name on it, but she said if I stuck around long enough that I'd get my own), and then she showed me the stack of gray plastic bins that I'd have to use to put all of the dirty plates and cups and silverware that people left behind at their tables.

"After you fill this thing up," she said, "take it back to the kitchen and Chance will show you how to use the dishwasher."

"Okay," I said. I picked up one of the bins from the top of the stack and set it against my hip. But before I was halfway out the kitchen, Ms. Cindy stopped me. "Don't forget this," she said as she tossed me a dirty rag. "You got to wipe out the booths and clean the tables off, too. Some of these people that come in here are nasty as hell. You wouldn't believe it."

But I did.

The first dirty table I went to was covered with greasy plastic plates, forks, knives, and cups, the leftover Pepsi turned a pale brown from the melted ice. There were damp, crumpled up napkins stuffed in some of them and a few half-eaten slices of pizza left on the aluminum tray in the center of the table. Everything seemed to be layered with grease, which had turned a sort of red-orange color from the pepperoni slices that had been mostly picked off and eaten.

I looked around the dining room to see if anyone was watching me. For some reason, I felt embarrassed to be cleaning off this table, but it was my job, and I was getting paid for it. The arcade games beeped and hummed in the dining room, and I could see the lights from the claw machine and the jukebox, which was playing a Garth Brooks song through the cracked overhead speakers that pocked the ceiling and seemed to float among the bars of fluorescent lighting and coffee-colored water stains on the otherwise yellowed tiles. Ms. Cindy was still in the kitchen.

I set the bin on one of the seats and started clearing the table, putting the dirty dishes and trash into the bin and then wiping the surface with the damp rag that Ms. Cindy had handed to me. I picked up some straws and napkins from one of the seats—the cracked vinyl leaking its orange foam stuffing from the tiny fissures like clown hair—and then I saw something gray and wadded up in the corner next to the tinted window that was lit by a flickering neon Bud Light sign and which was casting back my blurred reflection in the glass like a funhouse mirror.

I had to crawl toward the back of the booth to reach it, and when I put my hand out to grab whatever it was, I felt something damp. I looked around again to see if Ms. Cindy was watching me and wondered for a second if she had put this thing there to test me. I still didn't know what it was but after seeing Ms. Cindy was still in the kitchen, I turned and picked it up. It was a pair of gray wadded-up socks, darkened by moisture and maybe grease and maybe something else. I didn't even want to know what it was. Maybe the people who were eating here used them to wipe up a drink they'd spilled. Maybe it was their idea of a prank. Either way I just picked up the socks with the tips of my fingers and put them in the bin with all of the other trash.

When Chance passed by me on his way to the front door—he said he was leaving to go deliver some pizzas—he looked down in the bin at the pair of dirty socks on top.

"Those yours?" he said, smiling wryly. I couldn't tell if he was joking or not. Then his glance went down to my feet, obviously noting my shoes, and then he looked back up.

"People that come in this place are sick, man," he said. "You'll get used to it."

"Thanks," was all I could think of to say.

Then, he walked out of the door and into the night, the bell tinkling overhead as the door opened and closed behind him, a cloud of moths hovering in the wash of light from the security poles in the parking lot. I watched him climb into his truck and pull away. But I never did get used to that job. I quit a couple days later.

*

Not long after that, and for a couple of weeks during Christmas break, I lived with a good friend's older sister and her husband in their mobile home, which was squeezed into a crowded trailer park in Abita Springs, Louisiana. There were probably about forty trailers in rows of ten or twelve, each one no more than eight feet away from its neighbor. You could stand on the back porch, if you had one, and see right into the next person's windows. People fought constantly, and their fights would often spill out into the grassless lots, which were strewn with rusty bikes and old children's toys. A couple of abandoned cars provided refuge for the diapered babies who seemed to wander among the chaos like rats in a maze.

To pay my room and board there, I worked with my friend and his brother-in-law hanging drywall. We woke up in the mornings when it was still dark outside, tried to shake off our hangovers, walked out into the freezing cold, and squeezed into the little pickup truck that took us to our job. We stopped at Burger King or McDonald's for coffee and then drove in silence, the country music low in the background as the tires rolled along the blacktop, the often-desolate landscape spooling out around us.

Usually, nobody said much of anything that early in the morning, but once, Charles, our foreman, pointed out a trailer back in the woods as we were driving to the construction site where we were working that day. He told us when he was about fifteen or sixteen, he stayed in that trailer with an older woman—she was probably in her late twenties or early thirties at the time, he said—while the woman's husband worked offshore on one of the oil rigs in the Gulf of Mexico. He was expected to be gone for two weeks.

"But for some reason," Charles said, "this dude came home early. Found me in his house with his old lady and beat the shit out of me. I'll never forget that."

My friend and I listened and watched the trailer that Charles was telling us about disappear into the woods as we drove farther and farther down the road.

"I tell you what, though," Charles said, "I tried to fight him back, but I couldn't make my damn hands into fists. You ever have that happen? When it's too early in the morning or too cold outside and you can't make a good fist?"

I tried to make a fist with my right hand to see what he was talking about, but my fingers—he was right—just wouldn't close all the way. It was too cold outside still, or too early in the morning.

"You always gotta be ready to fight," he said. "Even if it's in the morning, just grab you a bat or something, man."

*

There was a sort of hierarchy that existed in that job: the newest person (me, in this case) was constantly picked on and ridiculed. I couldn't do anything right. My measurements were always wrong, I climbed up the scaffolding wrong, I held my tools wrong, I was the one who dented the sheetrock when we carried it down a studded corridor, squeezing past the tufts of pink insulation pulled taut in places by the still-exposed wires and PVC pipes. It was constant, the criticism, but I couldn't quit, couldn't let them see they bothered me. In my case, even at fifteen years old, I was working to support myself and to have a place to live.

My hands hurt, my head hurt, I was tired, but still, at the end of the day, I was expected to go back to that trailer and keep up with everyone else in how much alcohol I consumed, how much pot I smoked, how much partying I did and crude jokes I told. And the next morning we would do it all over again. It was perseverance in the darkest sense. My other choice was to go back home and face my stepdad, who I knew had been looking for me. I was afraid of what he might do when he finally found me.

Then, one night he did.

We had all been drinking, and he pulled up to the bald lot in front of the trailer and dumped all my belongings into the yard. It had just rained so my clothes and books were soggy when I finally came outside to collect them. My stepdad never came inside or tried to talk to me. I was glad for that, at least.

My friend and his sister helped me to drag my clothes inside, and we stuffed everything into the dryer, even though they still had mud and dirt on them from being in the yard. The guitar my stepdad had tossed was broken, its neck dangling from the now-loose strings like a broken bone. We threw that away. The only other thing I had, besides my books, was an old IBM Selectric typewriter. It weighed twenty-five pounds, and it smelled strongly of the oil that I had used to lubricate the keys. Now, it had water and clumps of grass inside of it, so I counted it as another loss and pitched it into the dumpster along with my ruined guitar. I left the books out on the porch to dry.

I lived in that trailer for another week or so, hanging drywall every day, until the Christmas holidays were over and I had to go back to school. I went back home to live with my stepparents—I just couldn't do it on my own anymore—and I remember that my stepdad actually seemed glad I had worked hard during the break. He didn't say anything about me not being home for nearly a month as I went into my room with a couple of Wal-Mart bags filled with my clothes and books. He never asked about the typewriter or my guitar. Things like that, and what they were used for, had no purpose in his world.

*

Before I finally went to college, I floated by with a number of different jobs: a telephone operator, a caretaker in a park, and a stint in a factory belonging to Toland Enterprises, where I pressed designs onto flags, rugs, and mats for eight hours a day. I got that job during the first summer after I finished high school. By this time, my stepdad had lost his own job as an electrician. He had been drinking during his lunch breaks, missing whole days of work, showing up late. He had some serious jail time hanging over him for multiple DWIs, and I had to help out my stepfamily with the bills. And this job was the best I could do.

But it was probably the hardest job I ever had. I worked from four in the afternoon until 12:30 in the morning. It was in the middle of the summer, and the factory was cooled by large fans that only served to move stale, hot air around, never actually cooling anything off. The ink from the large presses made the air feel burnt and thick. It hurt your throat and lungs. Those hot machines burned your fingers, and the dark ink stained your skin.

My job in that factory was to stand in front of one of those large metal presses and place blank pieces of fabric onto a brown, rubber-matted surface, and then hold down the wooden handle of the machine for about thirty seconds until an image was stamped onto the material. I used a stencil, and every so often, I had to replace the stencil with a new design.

I was responsible for making things like American flags, oversized sunflowers with a tiny gray kitten poking out from between the bright green stems, a "Welcome" sign, and one that said, "Life is Better at The Lake." I wondered who bought these things, and I would fantasize about the kind of life one must have in order to appreciate something like this.

The machine became hotter over the course of my shift. It radiated heat, and steam emanated from its sides each time I pressed the lid down. The thing seemed alive, angry. A couple of times I burned my fingers on it. I envied the man whose job it was to use a forklift to move empty boxes into a trash compactor that was as big as a dumpster. I thought if I stayed here long enough, though, I could do his job. Anything would be better than standing in front of this machine all evening and into the night and early morning hours.

*

We had a thirty-minute, unpaid lunch break, but we weren't allowed to leave the premises to eat. I never planned ahead enough to bring my own food, so after I clocked out, I sat in the wainscoted break room and ate peanuts from a vending machine. I drank water because it was free. I drank cold, stale coffee from a Styrofoam cup while some of the other workers slept with their heads resting on their arms on the long picnic table in the middle of the room.

One night, I was working next to an older man named Ted. You had to keep count of how much you produced. If your numbers didn't increase or you didn't meet a certain quota each night, you were let go. So Ted was trying to help me get my quota up on this particular night.

He told me about how he had three daughters and how his wife had left them all one day. Just packed up and left. He said he was working this night job to keep up with all the bills. He worked as a mechanic during the day.

"When do you sleep?" I asked him.

He looked at me and laughed. "I don't," he said.

I thought about my stepdad at home, not working, lying on the sofa with a Budweiser in his lap, a cigarette burning in the ashtray on the coffee table. Watching movies. I told myself I wanted to be like this man here: enduring, strong, steadfast. Ted was a father who would do anything for his kids.

But not all the workers in the plant were like Ted. Some were temporary employees placed there by a temping agency, others were just drifting from job to job. People walked out mid-shift every day. They just left. They got into their cars and they pulled away. The foreman was so used to this happening that he never told these employees anything. He'd just watch them go.

Once, this guy Curtis walked out to the parking lot during his lunch break and started ambling around his car. I had stepped out of one of the large bay doors for a cigarette and could see him standing there, then milling around a bit. He was looking back at the warehouse, and I could tell he was thinking about leaving. I thought I was the only person watching him. But after a minute or two, when he just got in his car and started it up, a couple of people laughed, maybe one or two even clapped for him, and then he pulled out into the gravel road in his dirty, white Honda Civic. It was dusk by then. I could see his taillights coming together into a single point of light as he went down the road. The dust cloud his wheels kicked up behind him turned red before settling back down over the long weeds in the ditch.

I left that evening, and each one after it, feeling exhausted and numb. Then, I woke up one afternoon and decided I wasn't going to go in that day, nor any day after. I had to find something else.

No one from that place ever called to see where I was, to ask if I was coming back. I simply received a check in the mail for the hours I had put in. I knew I had done nothing for them that couldn't be done as well or better by someone else.

*

A couple of years later, I got a job as a draftsman. It was in an air-conditioned office, and I was able to sit the whole time while I worked up mechanical and electrical designs using an AutoCAD program: I got this job only because my grandfather was the president of the company, an engineering firm he had run since before I was born, and he was willing to pay me to learn. I was given the job if I promised I would go back to school while I worked there, which I eventually did.

And now here I am, telling you all of this, having made a career for myself as a writer and a teacher. I still can't believe it. But to me, it's important to remember that this writing is a human endeavor, and that people who have once done real work can also make books. Faulkner worked in a boiler room at Ole Miss. Larry Brown was a firefighter. Stephen King worked in an industrial laundry.

Writing is nothing mystical, nothing done by an elusive force. It is just another form of work, one that requires patience and perseverance and diligence, one that requires the endurance of pain and real experience. My hope is that perhaps someone will read about me on the back of one of my books and realize, as I did a while ago, that there is not always a clear path from one point of being to another. It is a tenuous strand of events, a tightrope walk that requires the utmost faith in the power of simple kinesis.

It is important to me that I worked hard, and at various things, before all these books could be made. It is important to me that I still hold onto those values of perseverance and hope and diligence no matter what I do in my life. It is important that we all work for something bigger than ourselves, and that it is our work, in whatever form it may take, that ultimately keeps us alive and even immortal. It is important there is meaning and hope to be found in those sometimes dark and awful places where we toil away and suffer Adam's eternal curse.

Connection

The first job I had where I wasn't washing dishes or busing tables in some greasy kitchen or sweating over a press in a hot warehouse in the middle of the night or waking up at dawn in the freezing cold to hang drywall was just after I finished high school and had dropped out of college. My stepdad had gotten fired from his own job and we needed the money, and I managed to find a job that paid $7.50 an hour, more than two dollars over the minimum wage in 1998.

It was a telemarketing place called Anserphone, only we didn't have to call our potential customers. They called us, ordering from the myriad catalog companies we had contracts with and that sold everything from high-end clothes to cigars to steaks to industrial supplies to Amish soap. But I wouldn't have cared either way. I was eighteen and this would be my first job indoors, with air-conditioning, tinted windows, a cubicle with a computer and telephone and my own headset so I could talk and type at the same time.

Before we could talk to actual customers, though, we had to go through a week of training. They told us that we would be paid for this, too. Another first in my experience.

I remember sitting in front of the computer that first day, the bright blue screen limning my hands and arms and face and the long fluorescent tubes humming softly overhead. I was in an otherwise quiet room with three or four trainees plus the lady who was going to teach us how to answer calls for these different companies and then how to enter the orders into our system for processing.

I was just happy to know that I would go home in the same clean clothes I was currently wearing, not covered in sweat and dirt and grease and needing a shower before I could get in my bed that night. I felt as if my life had finally taken a turn in the right direction.

Not to mention it was only two o'clock in the afternoon and I would be clocking out at 10:30 that evening. No sweeping or mopping or pulling out trash. Just stamp my card and walk out to my dusty Ford Taurus and go home. The thought was invigorating.

"Good afternoon, y'all," the trainer said as she walked into the room, pulling the door shut behind her. You could hear the suction of air as it pushed up on the large ceiling tiles and then the sound as they settled softly back into place. "My name is Keisha and I'm going to be teaching y'all all about our company and what we do here. By the end of this week," she said, "you'll all be ready to go out on the floor and answer phones for these catalogs and will probably know more about their products than the owners themselves."

Keisha seemed cheerful and upbeat but not in a fake, put-on sort of way. She seemed genuinely happy to be there. We all gave her a polite laugh.

After we were finished introducing ourselves, Keisha passed around a stack of catalogs.

"Before we start," she said, "I want y'all to look these catalogs over and just try to familiarize yourselves with some of the products they have."

We each took one and started thumbing through the pages.

"The great thing about this job," she continued, "is that you don't have to *sell* any of this stuff. The customers actually call *us* to order it. Our job is basically just to assist them in placing the order so that the company can process it and get it shipped out."

The catalogs ranged in variety and appeal. One was for a company called Dr. Leonard's that sold things like walking canes, hearing aids, pill organizers, calculators, and alarm clock radios with oversized buttons and digital displays. A lot of their products were pictured next to a little red square with white lettering that said, "As Seen On TV."

Another was for a company called Paul Fredrick. They sold high-end dress shirts and ties for men. You could order a set of cuff links for seventy dollars, which seemed outrageous.

I was flipping through a catalog for Lehman's, who sold lanterns and soap and large, industrial-sized tubs in which you could store grains and rice, many months' worth, as well as water filtration systems and a lot of other large and very expensive products.

Keisha was standing over me as I pored over the photographs and prices. I couldn't imagine spending that much money on any one single thing, not to mention how much it cost to have it shipped to your house.

"We've been getting a lot of calls for them lately," she said, pointing at the catalog. "People who think the world's going to end in the year 2000. They're stocking up for it."

"Do you think it will?"

"What?" she said.

"That the world's going to end?"

"No," she said, "but I sure wish I owned a company like this one right now. I'd be a millionaire."

We passed around the catalogs. I tried to imagine the different types of people who would call to order these things, what they would say, how they would sound. If our exchanges would be simply pragmatic, or friendly, or if they would be rude, rushed, or mean.

I would soon learn that all of these scenarios would prove themselves true, in different ways, over the next year that I was able to keep that job. All before finally getting fired for manipulating the phone queue so that I wouldn't have to take as many calls as some of the other people who worked there.

*

A few of those people I worked with at Anserphone that year became my friends. After all, I was working eight- to ten-hour shifts, five to sometimes seven days a week, and it seemed as though I saw them more than my own stepfamily.

There was Paul, a guy about my age, whose dad, he told me, was a Baptist preacher. He lived with his parents in a dusky trailer right across from the small, brick church where his father preached. There was a narrow gravel walkway that went from the front double doors of the sanctuary over a patch of thick green grass to the wobbly metal staircase leading up to his trailer. It was single-wide, aluminum, just like the one I lived in.

At certain times in the day, Paul told me, the sun would cast a shadow from the large wooden cross on the church's steeple in a perfect line over that gravel path and right to their trailer's front door.

"It's like Jesus is trying to get in every day," Paul said, laughing. Paul had a slightly awkward way about him, so I wasn't always sure how to take the things he told me. Was he trying to be funny, or was he serious?

I just smiled and stood at the front of the steps that day on our lunch break as I waited for him to go inside and get something he said he'd forgotten. He hadn't told me what it was. But his mom had asked that I not come in, and I remember her poking herself out from the darkened threshold to say hello.

"Sorry to make you stand out here like this," she said. "It's just that my husband's asleep and I don't want to wake him up."

"That's okay," I said. "I understand."

When Paul emerged, his mother kissed him on the cheek. "I love you, honey," she told him.

He didn't say anything back, just hopped over the staircase and onto the grass. He told me to come on. Our lunch break was only thirty minutes and we had to hurry back to avoid clocking in late.

"Bye," I said to his mom, following Paul back to his car. "It was nice to meet you."

"It was nice meeting you, too," she said quietly, almost a whisper from where she stood within the darkened opening to her trailer. She waved to me, and her face looked very pale and sad from where she was standing.

When Paul and I got back to work, we had about five minutes left of our lunch break. Neither one of us had any money to get lunch, so we just sat on the trunk of his car in the gravel parking lot. A couple of people were standing around the side entrance, smoking cigarettes and drinking coffee from little Styrofoam cups. It was getting dark outside. You could already hear the grasshoppers and the frogs and the crickets buzzing in the weeded ditch behind the lot.

Then after a few minutes the people standing around outside started flicking their cigarettes and trudging back in. Lunch was over.

*

Most of the calls I took while I worked at Anserphone were about what you'd expect. Typical. People placing orders, people calling to complain about orders they hadn't received or about items they received but weren't happy with. People wanting more information about a product before buying it.

Sometimes they were interesting though. Like the callers who insisted on knowing where I was located (I wasn't allowed to tell them) before they'd do business with me. Or the ones who tried to use fake credit card numbers to place extravagant orders. We always had to complete the process and then cancel the order after the customer was off the phone. We were to avoid confrontations at all costs.

But sometimes people would call just to talk. They sounded lonely. Desperate for any kind of conversation, human interaction, no matter how remote or odd the context.

"Did anyone ever tell you how sexy your voice is?" a woman asked me once.

"No, ma'am," I said.

"Well, it is. You should get a job recording books on tape or something. I would pay *money* to hear your voice."

Then, she asked for my personal phone number. I told her we weren't allowed to give out that information.

She hung up on me.

The people I worked with were also interesting. There was a man named Russell, who was in his sixties, and who told me how he used to travel across the country in a van with his wife, doing farm work and odd jobs to afford food and diapers for their newborn child. This was before they knew Jesus and were saved, he said.

Was I saved? he always wanted to know.

There was Emily, an artist from New York who told me she used to be a ticket taker at a movie theater in the city when she was younger. Now that she was a grandmother, she said, one of her fondest memories was still the time when she and her college roommates each bought a pint of beer and drank them next to a lake in Central Park in the early afternoon.

I had never been to Central Park, or to New York, but I liked hearing that story. I liked Emily. She could have been my grandmother, and we would sit outside during our coffee breaks sometimes and talk. Every now and then, I'd bum one of her Misty cigarettes and just sit next to her, listening to her stories.

There was also Ed, a retiree who was still working full-time at the call center so that he could pay for his grandchildren to go to college. He relayed this information to me one day in a very dry, matter-of-fact way, as though this was what all grandparents did for their grandchildren. As if he was just reporting a fact, trying like everyone else here to connect with another human being.

And I still remember Larry, a young man who was going to be a Baptist minister, marry his high school sweetheart, and have lots of kids—a big happy family. Then he and his fiancée found out one day that they would never be able to have children, and I remember how quiet Larry was after that. He still wore a suit every day to work, sat in his cubicle, and took his calls. But you could tell there was something different about him.

I remember all these people, their stories, these threads of information and images going from one person to the next and then making their way to me—like the string we tied between two cans when we were kids so that we could hopefully hear one another from some imaginary distance. Which is all anyone ever really wants to do, isn't it? Connect with someone else. To say hello, I'm here, no matter how far apart they are. To have someone say back to them: I know. I can hear you.

*

During that year, I also became friends with a girl named Star and her best friend Jennifer. They lived out in the country like I did, and in trailers, and Star had gone out with one of my old friends from high school. The three of us liked a lot of the same music and would sometimes sit in my car during our breaks and listen to CDs, drink coffee, and smoke cigarettes.

Jennifer talked about her uncle a lot, how he lived with her and her dad and would sometimes flip out. He had been in Vietnam, she said.

"He just scares the hell out of me sometimes. Always yelling and throwing dishes against the wall in the middle of the night."

"That's why we're saving up," Star told me. "So we can get our own place soon. Get the hell out of Franklinton. Maybe you can move in with us."

"Yeah, that might be cool," I said. But I knew I could never do that. The money I was getting from that job all went to help keep our electricity on at home and to pay our other bills since my stepdad still wasn't working. On top of that, he was now also facing some serious jail time. I knew I couldn't leave. Even though I kind of wanted to.

But still I was young, and it was hard to take work seriously. I liked Star and Jennifer. I wanted to impress them, and for them to like me too. So, when Star told me one evening about how she and Jennifer would "push" calls down the queue by simply picking up their phone and hanging it right back up a second later, I started doing it too.

That way, we could go a whole hour without ever taking a call. I would sketch pictures in a little pad on my desk and we would all talk while everyone else worked. There were slow days too, of course, when hardly anyone would get a call. Times like that they'd let us read books or look at magazines. Some people would get sent home early.

Then, one evening the manager, Ms. Sandra, tapped me on the shoulder. "David?" she said. "Can you come with me to my office, please?"

"Okay," I said. I started to get up.

"Bring your stuff with you."

Star and Jennifer were both looking at their computer screens, acting busy. Neither one of them looked at me or Ms. Sandra as we walked away.

When we got to her office, Ms. Sandra asked me to sit down.

"Do you know what I wanted to see you about this evening?" she said.

"No, ma'am."

"It's about your call logs."

I didn't say anything.

"We keep track of all of that data, you know, and it seems as though you and a couple of your friends are logging significantly less calls than everybody else. Do you have any idea why that might be?"

"No, ma'am," I said. "Not really."

"Well. We didn't either at first. Then we looked at the average length of the calls you *were* taking and almost 90 percent of them were under two seconds long."

I still didn't say anything. There was nothing I could say. I felt stupid—not for getting caught, but for screwing up the first decent job I'd ever had. What would I do now? What would my stepfamily do? They needed me to have this job. Maybe, I hoped, I'd just get a warning this time.

Then, Ms. Sandra said, "We're going to have to let you go, David. I'm sorry."

"Yes, ma'am," I said. "I understand. I'm sorry too."

A few minutes later, while I was standing beside my car, the moonlight glazing the rocks on the parking lot so that they almost glowed white beneath my tennis shoes, Star and Jennifer came outside.

"Damn," Star was saying. "My mom's gonna freakin' kill me."

"Yeah, I know," I said. "This sucks."

Jennifer didn't say anything. I wondered if she was thinking about her uncle, screaming all night and breaking dishes against the wall in their cramped trailer.

Then Star wrote her number down on a sheet of paper, folded it up, and handed it to me. I put it in my jeans pocket.

"Call me sometime if you're ever in Franklinton," she said.

"Okay," I said. "I will."

I'm not sure why, but I never did call her. In fact, I never saw either one of them again.

*

When I got home early that evening, my stepdad wasn't as mad as I thought he would be that I lost my job. Maybe it was because he felt guilty that I was only nineteen and was working to pay all the bills that he should've been paying himself. Maybe it was because I told him I'd gotten laid off and not fired. I honestly hadn't known that there was a difference between the two terms until weeks later when filling out applications for a new job.

Which I eventually got. In another call center. But this time I'd be making the calls instead of taking them. Trying to sell stuff to people that they most likely didn't want and that they definitely didn't need.

My first day, I was handed a script that was about half a page long. I was told that all I had to do was call people from a list of numbers that I would find taped to my desk. There was no training at this job. I had to get on the phone as soon as I clocked in.

The script I was given told customers about a work-from-home job opportunity where they could earn up to eight hundred dollars a week stringing little plastic beads onto necklaces and bracelets. They could work their own hours and make as many or as little of the product as they wanted. The company would ship them all the materials and would pay the postage both ways. The customer only had to pay a one-time "start-up" fee of three hundred dollars to get going.

What the script didn't say was that it would probably take three people working twenty-four hours a day, seven days a week, to make enough of that jewelry to earn even half of what was being promised. It sounded too good to be true because it was. I knew it, and most of the people I called did, too.

I was hung up on, cursed out, laughed at, and rarely ever made it to the end of the script before the line was cut. Disconnected. But it was a job, and I needed the money. My stepfamily needed it.

In the three days I managed to stay at that place, I had only one customer who seemed sincerely ready to give me her credit card number. She seemed genuinely excited by the prospect of working from home, making her own hours. She sounded so eager, in fact, that at first I thought she was just getting a kick out of stringing me along and was planning on hanging up on me right at the end. Fifteen minutes wasted. But maybe she was just like some of the other people I had talked to, someone just wanting a connection with another person. Those fifteen minutes could have been very important to her. Maybe that's all I really had to give anyway, my time.

Still, she asked a lot of questions, ones I answered by simply reading the text on the page in front of me. (We didn't have computers at this call center, just an old phone in the middle of a scuffed-up desk.)

After a while, she finally seemed satisfied that all her concerns had been addressed. Then, she told me that this call was like a miracle, an answered prayer.

"My husband's in prison," she said. "Me and our kids are living at Mama's house, but I can't work and be home with the babies, too. Mama works right now, but we can barely afford to eat. I been prayin' and prayin' somethin' would come along like this. Then you just called me up. It's a miracle. I almost didn't even answer the phone, but this here just proves that Jesus is real."

I didn't say anything. I didn't know what to say. There was nothing in the script to address something like that.

I guess I could've just reaffirmed that she was making the right choice for her and her family, and even though three hundred dollars wasn't necessarily easy to come by, it was an investment in their future. Then nudge her again for her credit card number, like I had been told to do on the script.

But it just didn't feel right. None of it did. It felt more dishonest than pushing those calls off on my coworkers at Anserphone.

So I just waited.

"So, it's just this one-time fee, right?" she said, a sense of apprehension starting to creep back into her voice. I knew it was because of my silence, as though she could sense my own reservations through that phone line. I was transmitting my feelings to her now, and likewise her to me.

It was as if we could really sense each other, like a true communication.

Finally, I said, "Yes, ma'am. Just the one fee upfront."

"And I can make as much of these necklaces as I want to?"

"Yes, ma'am. There's no limit. You determine your own production." That phrase was right from the script.

"And there are absolutely no other fees or costs, right?"

"Yes, ma'am, that's right."

"I just want to be 100 percent sure," she said. "This is money that would otherwise be going to food for my two babies. Rent. Clothes. Gas."

Silence. I wondered if she could hear me breathing through the receiver.

"Well, okay then," she said. "And I can call this same number back if I need to speak with you? The number that showed up here on my caller ID?"

"Yes, ma'am. Someone will always be here to take your call. If not me, it will be someone else."

"Well, all right then. I guess I'll use a Visa card. Are you ready?"

"Yes, ma'am. Go ahead."

My hand was shaking as I held the pencil over the space next to her name for the credit card information.

"Okay. The number is 4, 1, 2—"

But before she finished, I reached out and pressed my index finger on the button in the phone's plastic cradle and disconnected the call.

Ghosts in the Mountains

Let me start off by saying this: I never wanted to go to the Sewanee Writers' Conference in Sewanee, Tennessee. I didn't want to leave my family for two weeks, didn't want to be alone with a bunch of strangers, didn't want to be away from my daily, at-home routine. But I have a lot of good friends who work on offshore oil rigs, and this is exactly what they do every month. They leave their homes, their families, their routines, for two weeks at a time, so I considered myself pretty lucky to be doing this just so I could go write and talk about writing at a beautiful college campus in the mountains.

Before I went there, I imagined being surrounded by a bunch of sycophantic, wannabe writers, struggling to keep my dignity while meeting with editors and agents and other writers who have "made it" (whatever that means) and not really knowing what I wanted from them or why I was there among them in the first place. Of course, everyone wants to meet that person who can bolster their career, who will recognize something in the work that sparks a fire of inspiration and dedication, thus spurring them on (whether they be an agent or editor or fellow author) in a rush of promotion and high praise. But I didn't know if I was ready for that: talking to folks—let's face it, complete *strangers*—about my books, selling my work and myself in the process. This is what I thought Sewanee was going to be like. But as I have been many times before in my life, I was wrong.

For the first day or two, I kept to myself mostly, feeling things out, getting a sense of the people who were there with me, and trying to focus on my then novel-in-progress, *The Gorge*. It was going to be my third book, and I was heavy into editing and revising and organizing it. I was trying to gear myself up for two weeks of this type of work, a sort of self-imposed literary boot camp, with the hope that I would have a complete draft of the book in hand by the time I got home. I didn't know that I would come away with not only a finished book, but with a sense that I had been in the mountains for those two weeks among many, variegated spirits who would continue to inspire me and my work, even as I sit here writing this.

I didn't know that spirits haunted the mountains of Sewanee. And when I say "spirits," of course, I don't mean the literal specters that you see in horror movies or Edgar Allan Poe stories. But there are spirits there, nonetheless. Ghosts. They come alive in the woods over booze and cigarettes, someone bringing up Barry Hannah or William Gay in conversation, two literary giants whose ghosts still linger in the pines like river fog. You can almost see William Gay standing against the bole of one of those pine trees, smoking a Marlboro Light and looking down at his ratty sneakers, hardly the image one might conjure when thinking of a writerly talent like his. With his long, greasy hair and gray, pointed mustache, he looks more like the drywall hanger, sometimes-carpenter, sometimes-housepainter that he had once been during his apprenticeship as a writer.

I met Amy Williams, William Gay's former agent, and we talked about Gay and his work as the sun went down behind those tall pines that jutted out of the precipice like long black paintbrushes, scrubbing at the orange and violet sky as if it were itself a blurred canvas. I swear it felt as though he was there listening to us. But it was a comforting feeling to have.

I also met Tim O'Brien, the guy who wrote *The Things They Carried*, which was the book that made me realize I wanted to be a writer back when I was in college. I mean, how many times do you get to say something like that in your life? I'll never forget a reading he gave one evening, where he read from an essay he had written about being a seventy-something-year-old father to two young sons. Both his boys were in the audience, which of course made me miss my own kids that much more, and as O'Brien read about his own father, his experience in Vietnam, eventually becoming a writer, then a father late in his own life, he finally read something like, "But I'll never live to see my sons' twenty-ninth birthdays." It was just a mathematical fact, but still you could hear the gulp in his throat as he tried to make it through the rest of the paragraph, and you could see some of the audience look over at O'Brien's kids, probably to see what their reaction would be to hearing something like that. And I remember those two little boys just sat there looking up at their dad as he wept in front of two hundred strangers.

But the math was right: since O'Brien himself was in his seventies at the time, it was unlikely he'd be around another twenty years to see his boys grow up to be adults. How do you not hear something like that, something

"Well, I have some of you want to go smoke it later."

"Okay," I said.

Then, he got up and I just sat there for a while, looking out at the sun as it disappeared behind the line of trees and the sloping hills in the distance.

When it was finally dark, I got up and started walking back to my room, which was on the other side of campus and down a meandering path of sidewalks and trails that cut through the woods in places, past stone houses and large, shadowed buildings, the moonlight washing over them like sprays of water cascading down the side of a gorge.

I could see the light from someone's cell phone up ahead of me, and whomever it was must have heard me because they stopped walking and turned around. It was James.

"Hey, man," he said. "What's up?"

"Not much. Just headed back to my room."

"You still wanna smoke that joint?" he said.

"Yeah, man, I guess." I hadn't smoked pot in years, and I felt kind of stupid for even thinking about doing it now, but then I thought it might help break the ice.

"Cool," he said. "We can just go down that trail up there." James pointed ahead with the light from his phone. "There's a field past those woods. I walked out there last night. It's quiet."

"All right," I said. "That sounds good to me."

When we got to the trail, we turned off from the sidewalk and went down a steep embankment and into a dark canopy of trees. Then, we walked deeper and deeper into the woods, the trail narrowing and falling off into slabs of rock on either side of us. It was so dark now you could hardly see your hands in front of your face, and at some point, I had to get out my phone and use its flashlight to see where we were going.

"It's coming up," James said. "Just keep going straight, man."

I thought about the time my friends and I had eaten mushrooms in high school and had sneaked onto a football field before getting picked up by the cops. How, twenty years later, was I still doing the same dumb shit? *Maybe I should just go back*, I thought, *call my wife and kids. Go to bed.*

"You all right?" James said.

"Yeah, this is cool," I said. "It's just hard to see back here."

"Yeah, no shit. It's like *Deliverance* or something," he said.

"Man, I hope not."

He laughed.

When we got to the field, it was lit up with streams of moonlight and you could look out at the sky, which stretched forth beyond the hills and trees and rocks and was prickled with stars and smears of blue-gray clouds. We crossed the field and went over to some more woods on the other side. Then, we sat down on a cool slab of rock and James took off his backpack and pulled out his pack of Kools.

"Want one?" he said.

"Yeah, thanks."

He handed me a cigarette and I lit it with his cheap Bic. Then he shook out a tiny rolled-up bag from the cigarette pack and used a book as a flat surface to roll a joint under the light from his phone.

When he was done, he lit it and took a long hit, held it in for a minute, then passed the joint over to me. It'd been years since I'd gotten high, so after just a few hits I could already feel it. My head felt as if it were completely stuffed with gauze. My eyes were dry. I lay back down on the cool shelf of rock and looked up through the skeletal branches fingering the sky, the scant light from my phone and the occasional flick of the lighter brushing up against them like one of those old fluttering gas flames in a theater playing over the silhouettes of the actors on the stage.

I could hear the crickets and the frogs buzzing and croaking and chirping somewhere off in the woods and James typing something on his phone next to me, the little clicking noises it kept making. He was smoking another cigarette and looking at something on his phone's blue screen. The slab of rock pressed into my spine. After a while, we both got up and walked back through the woods to our dorms.

"Thanks for the joint," I told him.

"Yeah, no problem," he said.

Then, I went into my room and fell asleep. And I didn't have any nightmares.

*

The next day I skipped out on the readings and lectures and meetings to visit with my uncle who had driven down to Tennessee from Ohio. I had sent him an email the week before I left for the conference to see if he'd want to hang out while I was there, especially since it would be about the same distance from where both of us lived.

I hadn't seen my uncle since just before he left Louisiana after Hurricane Katrina flooded his house in New Orleans. He and my aunt had lost almost everything in the storm, and all he had left fit into a small U-Haul, which he had hitched to the back of his car one day and drove north. That had been almost ten years ago.

But he had emailed me back and said he'd love to see me again. We had been incredibly close when I was a kid and I looked up to him like a father figure. I remember wanting to be just like him when I was younger. He was an artist and an actor but had this masculine vibe about him too. People used to say he looked like Patrick Swayze, which he did.

Now, he was calling me on my cell phone to say he'd just pulled up.

I walked outside as he was getting out of his car and went over to hug him.

"Hey, man," he said.

"Hey, Ted," I said. "You look good, man." I squeezed his upper arm, which had become even more lean and muscled since the last time I had seen him. I knew he lived on a farm now, raising goats and doing mostly outdoor manual labor, so it was good to see him looking so young still, and healthy.

"Damn, I can't believe how long it's been," he said.

"I know. I'm glad you're here, man."

I knew I'd miss a good part of the conference now that my uncle was there, but I didn't really care about that anymore. It was just so good to connect with someone from my family again, even if the circumstances weren't ideal.

My uncle and I walked inside and went to the bar. He ordered a screwdriver, which is what he'd always had ever since I can remember. I ordered a beer. We sat and talked until the bartender told us he was closing up soon.

I told Ted about my mother (his older sister) and her suicide attempt, how she'd lived with me and my family, and how I'd since stopped speaking to her. I told him about my own family, whom he'd never met. I showed him some pictures of my wife and children on my phone. After Katrina, we'd lost touch with each other, and now it was like trying to fit all of those years into just a few short hours. But we tried.

We talked nonstop, it seemed, leaving the bar and eventually driving to a Waffle House just off campus, where we sobered up and ate and smoked one after another from his pack of Winstons. At one point, I went to the bathroom and coughed into the sink and was shocked that my spit was black from all the tar and smoke.

*

On my last morning at Sewanee, as I was walking from my dorm room and to the inn, where I would tell my uncle goodbye and then get on a bus that would take me to the airport, I saw a family of deer on the sidewalk just in front of me. No cars were out, the air was cool, and the sky was gray and wet. It is the best time of day to walk and to think, especially in the Tennessee mountains. The deer were nosing around in the grass, seemingly unaware of my approach, their eyes like large oil spots on their smooth, tan-and-white faces. I set my bags down on the sidewalk and tried to slip my phone from my pocket so that I could get a picture of them, but just like that, they were gone—off into the woods in about two quick leaps that were as silent as breath, their forms completely disappearing into the foggy early morning dark of that ghostly and majestic place.

Independence Day,
Part Two

I t was almost dark outside when the mushrooms finally started to kick in. We had picked a Wal-Mart bag full of them earlier that afternoon from a muddy cow field in Goodbee, Louisiana, but not before being chased across the pasture, jumping over fallen branches and stumps that were camouflaged by tall weeds and red ant piles, getting our clothes and jeans torn by the rusted barbed wire fence as we squeezed between the strands and fell onto the gravel road, making it back to my beat-up Mazda B2200 pickup truck and barely getting it started before about four or five farmers caught up to us with their loaded black shotguns, yelling and spitting brown streams of tobacco juice from their angry red faces as we pulled away from them in a cloud of dry, gray dust.

We were sweating and laughing, knowing we had just barely escaped something potentially horrible, and still hoping the men hadn't thought to write down our license plate number or, worse, to start firing at us with their twelve-gauges as we sped away into the shade of pine trees that lined the side of that otherwise quiet country road.

My friend Mike was riding shotgun and Gary was in the middle of the bench seat, the stick shift ramming into his thigh as I changed gears to get us out of there and back onto the highway. I lit a cigarette from the slightly damp pack of Camels sitting on the cracked dashboard and then rolled down my window to let the smoke out. Mike and Gary each lit one, too.

"Shit," Mike said. "That was crazy."

He leaned over Gary a little bit and flicked on the radio. It was an old Alpine tape deck I had bought from a pawn shop and had shoved into the console, using some thick gray wires to hook up some house speakers, which I had squeezed in behind the seats. You had to keep the bench seat pushed close to the dashboard so that your knees were always cramped up underneath it, but it was the only way to get music in there.

When my stepdad first bought that truck ten years earlier, it was a stripped-down model: no A/C, no power steering, no radio. Now the odometer had been completely turned over, the tailgate had fallen off, the back bumper was dented up to the wheel well, and the windshield had cracks spread across its surface like rivers on an old, crumpled map.

The tape spooled slowly through the metal capstan and the speakers buzzed behind us before 311's "Homebrew" finally came on—the low distorted guitar and bass trembling through the sweaty cab and under our muddy tennis shoes like a steady current of warm, gushing water.

It was the Fourth of July. And, like the song said, we would never be the same.

And it was probably from the LSD we had done the year before that. I remember it was on a little square of white paper that fit right in the center of my fingertip. The paper looked thicker than normal, almost like construction paper, and I could see my fingerprint behind it as though I were looking at everything through a magnifying glass. I looked at it for a good while before finally placing it on my tongue and then driving onto Highway 25. We had been sitting in my little Mazda pickup truck in the parking lot of a Shell station in Covington and were about to head to my girlfriend's parents' camp just north of Folsom so that we could trip without being disturbed by anyone. I was sixteen years old.

I didn't want to take the acid until we got to the camp because I was afraid it would kick in while I was driving, and since I had never done acid before, I wasn't sure how it would affect me. But Mike had assured me it wouldn't take effect until well after we were at the camp, so I put the paper square on my tongue and drove off. Lisa, my girlfriend at the time, sat in the middle of the bench seat with her leg pressed against the stick shift and some of our other friends followed behind us in a different car.

The camp was in the woods somewhere north of Folsom, and there were cow pastures and horse fields all around us. Tall pines jutted out from the ground on either side of the gravel road, where deep ditches lay like some giant's ax marks in the hard, clay earth. When we finally pulled up, it was nearly dark out, so we all went inside to look around.

The acid started to take effect slowly, and I remember the first feeling of something being different was a dull throbbing in my lower spine—it wasn't unpleasant, but it felt strange, as though someone was pressing a hard pillow in the middle of my back. Then, sounds started to become altered. I could hear what seemed to be a flock of geese off in the dark woods somewhere, their wings rustling against their bodies and the sound of their webbed feet in the mud. Occasionally, you could hear one of them quack or pull a strand of grass from the ground. Each sound and movement was magnified.

Light began to vibrate, as though someone had plucked a string that was tied between two walls. The woods around us seemed to pulse, the green of each leaf brighter than it normally would have been, each drop of condensation more magnified so that you could almost see the particles of dirt inside of it.

Lisa and I were walking through the woods by then, the wet grass coming up to our thighs and the moonlight coming down through the branches and turning into spiderwebs on our greasy skin. I kept hearing what sounded like those geese, or maybe they were ducks, but Lisa told me she couldn't hear anything. I looked at her face, and it looked as though someone was holding a blacklight in front of her: her skin looked pale and her teeth and the whites of her eyes looked brighter than normal. Whiter than a sheet of paper. There was an outline of light around her body that seemed to pulse like a small engine humming in the distance.

Then, we heard a car coming down the gravel road behind us. I looked at Lisa and grabbed her by the arm and we sort of rolled over onto the side of the road and into the ditch. Branches cut my arms and tore holes in my shirt. Our faces were close together and I put my head down into the mud and we stayed that way until the car passed by on the road, spreading a cloud of dry dust over us like a threadbare sheet.

After we climbed out of the soggy ditch, Lisa and I walked back to her parents' camp. Where everyone had once been hanging out in the carport was now empty, only the single naked bulb casting down its yellow light on the grease-stained concrete where her parents parked their cars but on which we had put some metal fold-up chairs to sit on earlier. They were all empty now.

"Where is everybody?" she said.

"I don't know." I looked around, disoriented and feeling a swell of anxiety creeping up from my stomach and into my throat, as though I were about to throw up.

Then, Mike ran up, seemingly from out of the black curtain of pine trees that surrounded the house, as though he had materialized out of those woods. He told us that someone was chasing him with a shotgun, some old man, and that everyone else had scattered off into the horse fields.

"Oh, my God," Lisa said. "Shit."

"What are we going to do, man?" I said.

"Just run. I don't know. Hide somewhere."

"Where is he?" Lisa said.

"Who?"

"The man with the shotgun."

"I don't know," Mike said. "He just ran through the house and then went out the back door. Everybody ran."

"Let's go hide in the house," I said. "Get out of the light."

I took Lisa's hand, and we went into the house. It was wrecked. Beer cans and half-empty whiskey bottles were strewn across the cracked linoleum floors, tables and chairs were turned over on their sides, the sliding glass door was wide open, a pair of antlers was lying in the threshold.

We went through one of the bedroom doors and over the mess on the floor and then into a dark closet in the corner of the room. I looked behind us and Mike was still there, waiting to get in the closet with us. We all three crouched inside and pulled the door shut behind us. Now, we couldn't see anything. I could hear our own breathing and feel the closed space getting warmer from our bodies.

"What the hell?" I said.

"I know," Mike said. "This is fucked up," he said. Then, he started laughing.

We heard someone in the house. They were kicking around some of the stuff on the floor and yelling for us to come out. The voice was loud and grizzled-sounding and slightly out-of-sync with everything else.

Lisa whispered that she knew who that was. It was the old man who lived down the road. He knew her parents. She told us that we should just go out and tell him we broke into the house, but that she would stay hidden so her parents wouldn't find out she was here.

"No way," Mike said.

"Yeah, let's just wait until he leaves," I said. "He won't come back here."

And this turned out to be a good idea, too, because eventually the old man left.

*

We were exhausted, but it wasn't until around five in the morning when we finally lay down to try to get some sleep. I was still wired from the LSD, but I climbed in one of the lower bunk beds with Lisa and closed my eyes. The rising dawn light was coming in through one of the windows, and it spread out across my eyelids so that I could see the veins inside of them. They pulsed with each one of my heartbeats and were bright red and circuitous. Within the myriad crooked lines in my eyes I could see what looked like flower petals, but they were magnified to the point that each drop of moisture was visible on their leaves and they twitched in the breeze like a split film reel clicking through a projector whose motor has overheated and then I could feel the warmth of it next to me, so I kicked the blanket off and moved toward the wall and away from Lisa.

Which felt strange, because just a few months before that, I think I lost my virginity to her, but now I'm not so sure. I remember we had all been doing drugs and drinking cheap bottles of Mad Dog 20/20 that night. It was the first time I met her.

We were at Gary's house, but everyone had slowly started to leave. The room where Lisa and I had been hanging out was dark now and someone had left on a CD so that music was playing low in the background. And now we were in the loft on top of a mattress and some pillows and a sleeping bag. As the last person left the room and pulled the door shut behind them, flicking off the light switch before disappearing onto the porch outside, Lisa leaned over and kissed me on the mouth—just like that, suddenly and unexpectedly. We moved closer to each other, and I started putting my hands up her shirt and pulling off her skirt. I remember the shock I felt at myself for doing this so quickly, but she didn't stop me, and the alcohol and the pot were further emboldening me to keep going. We kept kissing each other, breathing heavily and sweating.

I could taste the weed and the alcohol on her mouth, and my mouth was dry as I kissed her. It was dark so I could barely see her face until a curtain of light crossed over us as someone opened the door and came back into the room. It was Mike. He looked up to where Lisa and I lay tangled up in the loft. Then he laughed as we pulled away from each other and leaned over the side to look down at him. There were a few condoms strewn across the floor and Mike bent down and picked one up and tossed it up into the loft. He looked embarrassed. Then, he flicked the light switch off and left the room again.

Now it was dark, and Lisa and I started to kiss each other some more, then I felt up her shirt, then she took mine off. I started to take off my jeans. We were sweating and holding each other's bodies close, breathing each other's warm air.

"Put that little sucker on," Lisa said, pointing with her chin at the condom that was lying next to us on the sheets. She was breathing hard, and I could see the whites of her eyes and the pale skin on her face as she looked up at me. I picked through the sheets and pillows and blankets and clothes until I had the condom and then I opened the package and tried to put it on. But I couldn't see too well in the dark and I was nervous, shaking, so I did a poor job of it. Lisa stopped me.

"I'll be right back," she said. "I have to pee."

"All right," I said.

After she climbed out of the loft, I turned over on my back and looked up at the ceiling. It was slanted down and only about a foot or so from where I lay. Someone had painted on it, and I tried to make out the painting until Lisa came back. I saw the light coming out from the bathroom and heard the door close after she went inside; then a few seconds later, I heard the toilet flush and the door open, the light flooding back into the room before she flicked it off and started climbing back up the ladder and into the loft again. I was worried that it would be awkward when she came back up, but she immediately started to kiss me again and get on top of me, and then we rolled over until I was directly on top of her. She grabbed my hips and started to try to put me inside of her, but we weren't able to get very far. At some point the condom slid off and I couldn't get it back on right. Lisa was still breathing hard and kissing me on the neck and face and I tried to do what I was supposed to do but after a few minutes she stopped me. She said, "I think we're too drunk."

I pulled back from her, a little relieved. "Yeah," I said. We started to get dressed and dry the sweat from our bodies with the sheets and our clothes, and then we climbed down from the loft and went outside into the cool night air, where everyone else was sitting around a fire, like they had been waiting for us.

And now we lay in bed together, but at opposite sides of the mattress, in our own separate worlds, waiting for the effects of the LSD to subside enough so we could finally fall asleep. The sun was already almost fully out, though, and the hot white disk stabbed at my eyes through the window and poked at my throbbing skull. So, I got up and went outside, lit a Camel cigarette and held it loosely between my lips as we all started to pick up our garbage from the night before and put it in white plastic bags. Then, we threw them into the bed of my truck.

I was hungry and nauseous. I couldn't eat, hadn't slept, and couldn't order my thoughts, though the hallucinations had finally stopped. We all felt hungover, tired, depressed. The swath of land and the horse fields around us looked different now, as though we were in some fallen place. The trees looked darker too somehow, the blades of grass heavier and weighed down by the morning's condensation. We were dirty, we smelled bad. We just needed to get back home.

*

And now, not even a year after that experience, Mike and Gary and I had just finished picking about two dozen mushrooms, enough for a strong tea or for each of us to eat about eight of them—a good trip, Mike was saying as he counted them out onto the dashboard one by one.

Occasionally, I would glance over at the dirt-covered stems, the brown and almost purplish caps nearly glowing in the sheen of sunlight pouring in through the windshield.

As I finally turned off Brewster Road and onto the highway, there was a line of cars trailing down the road into the distant and far-off haze. They were stopped, their brake lights flashing on and off as they inched forward, moving one by one toward the roadblock up ahead, where about a half dozen police officers were checking driver's licenses and insurance cards, looking for drunks.

"Shit, man," I said. "What are we gonna do?"

"Don't worry," Mike said. "I got this." He reached down to the floor-board and picked up another Wal-Mart bag and pulled out some of the items we had purchased earlier that day—more cigarettes, a pack of gum, a loaf of white Bunny bread to soak up the contents of our stomachs if we got sick later.

I kept my foot on the clutch, easing the truck up the line to where the cops waited on either side of the road, their mirrored sunglasses reflecting the drivers' nervous faces as they passed their insurance cards, registration, and driver's licenses through their rolled-down windows and into the officers' waiting hands.

Mike was still busy with the groceries he had pulled from the bag, finally placing the loaf of Bunny bread onto the dashboard to cover the mushrooms.

"What the hell, man?" I said. "That's not gonna work. Put 'em under the seat or something. Hurry."

"Chill, don't worry about it," Mike said. "They're not gonna look under here."

But I wasn't so sure he was right. Just a couple of months before, when we were still in school, the cops came with their drug dogs to search backpacks and lockers and cars. They did this pretty regularly, and I remember some kids getting called out of the classroom, then being shaken down in the hall. It seemed like the cops never found anything, that it was more of a scare tactic than anything else.

But one of those times they called my name on the intercom.

"Send David Armand out to the hall, please," the voice said over the static.

"Yes, ma'am," the teacher said. Then to me, "David, go ahead. Bring your book sack."

"Okay," I said. I got up and walked into the hallway, where two cops were already standing there waiting.

"Come on, son," one of them said. "We're going out to the parking lot."

They flanked me, falling back as we went through the double doors at the end of the hall, then resumed their position on either side of me once we were outside the building.

When we got to the grass parking lot, they pointed to my truck. I had just gotten my license not long before and hadn't been driving long. It was my stepdad's old truck that he let us use to drive to school sometimes. "That Mazda yours?"

"Yes, sir," I said. "Well, it's my stepdad's, but he lets me use it."

"I thought it looked familiar," the cop said. "I know your stepdad. And not for anything good either."

The other officer laughed. "Well, son, we're going to need you to go over and open it up for us," he said.

"Why?"

"You don't ask questions here, you understand? You just do what we tell you."

"Yes, sir."

We kept walking over to the truck, where several other officers stood, one of them holding a K-9 on a leash. The dog pulled against him, trying to get closer to where my truck was parked. The principal was there, the vice principal, the disciplinarian.

"This your truck, son?" the officer holding the dog asked.

"Yes, sir," I said.

"Go ahead and open it up then. The dog hit on it, and we need to search it."

I went over to the driver's side door and unlocked it. The officer standing behind me immediately opened the door and reached down onto the floorboard, picking something up from the dirty spot near the brake pedal.

"What's this?" he said, holding something between his index finger and thumb, so close to my face that I couldn't see what he had.

"I don't know," I said.

"Well, it ain't an orange seed, son," the cop said. "It's pot. A marijuana seed." He went over to the other officer, who was holding a glass vial with some light blue liquid in it. Then, he dropped the seed he'd picked up into the vial.

"You smoke marijuana in here?" he said.

"No."

"We'll see about that."

The other officer was letting the dog into the truck now, and the animal was clawing up the seats and console, its tail wagging out through the open door.

"Yep, we got you," the officer with the vial finally said. He held it out so I could see it, showing me how the liquid inside had changed color. I didn't know what any of this meant. I was still trying to process what was going on.

The principal walked over, shaking her head and saying something into her walkie-talkie.

"This is an automatic expulsion, Mr. Armand," she said. "You know that, right? And you're lucky they don't take you in to the station."

I didn't say anything, just looked around and back toward my truck, from which the drug dog was now emerging, his handler shaking his head as well, but his was as if to say they hadn't found any drugs—just the one seed.

"We'll handle this from here," the principal was saying to the officer who was still holding the vial. "Mr. Armand, come with me," she said.

I followed her to the office, but I didn't get expelled from school that day. They just sent me home. It seemed like they had only wanted to scare me. I had long hair, I smoked cigarettes, and they knew who my stepdad was. It seemed like they just wanted me to know that they were watching me.

And now, here I was in the same truck, a couple of months later, approaching the cops' roadblock, but this time I did have drugs in the cab. Or at least I thought they were considered drugs.

Gary just snickered and then flicked his index finger at one of the knobs on the radio. The cassette tape that had been playing ejected from the slot in the console; Gary took it out and slid it under his leg. I wasn't sure why he did that. Maybe a little music going would've helped break the ice, calm the atmosphere for when the cop stuck his head in the cab.

It probably didn't matter.

All I could think of was what would happen if we got caught. I was pretty sure mushrooms were illegal, and I knew if one of those cops asked where we'd gotten them then we'd have to come up with something to say. That we'd trespassed on posted property, taken something from it that wasn't ours to take.

What if those farmers had already reported us, had sent in my license plate number? What if this roadblock had been set up just to catch us? What if I had to call my stepparents to tell them I'd been arrested? That I was in jail?

I was only sixteen and could hardly imagine these things happening to me. I started to wish I'd just stayed home.

All of these thoughts plowed through my head as we slowly approached the roadblock and its attendant officers dressed in black uniforms with long metal batons dangling from their belts that also held walkie-talkies, their guns, a flashlight.

The overhead lights on their cruisers were flashing blue and white and you could see them from where we were on the road. Occasionally, they'd pull someone out of the line and get them to drive onto the gravel shoulder of the highway for further inspection.

Then, they'd pop trunks, fling open back doors for their drug dogs to climb in. But they'd always send the car on its way, watching as it pulled off the dusty shoulder and into the haze, through which the dark gray string of highway seemed to disappear—a trembling and pulsing fog in the distance.

Now, it was our turn.

I eased up to the officer who was standing on the yellow centerline. I could see my reflection in his mirrored sunglasses as I looked out the window.

"You boys up to no good today?" he said. His close-mouthed smile was hardly visible beneath his thick brown mustache. You could see the spackling of gray hairs sprouting in there, too.

"No, sir," I said. "We're just going back home."

"And where might home be?"

"Covington."

"Y'all brothers?"

"No, sir. Just friends."

I looked over at Mike and Gary. They were both staring straight ahead and out through the cracked windshield. The loaf of bread in its yellow plastic wrapper still sat strangely on the dashboard, covering up our pile of damp mushrooms.

We waited.

"Y'all comin' back from the store or somethin'?" the officer said, glancing at the Wal-Mart bags on Mike's lap. There hadn't been enough room on the floorboard to keep them down there without his shoes crushing them.

"Yes, sir."

"Havin' a party for the Fourth?"

"No, sir."

"Too bad," the officer said. "But either way, I'm still gonna need to see your license and insurance and registration card."

"Yes, sir," I said.

I slid the gearshift to neutral, let my foot off the clutch and then pushed in the parking brake. I raised myself up from the torn bench seat and pulled my wallet from my back pocket, removed my license from the plastic sleeve, and passed it through the window to the officer.

As he was examining it, I leaned over and clicked open the glove compartment and pulled out the insurance and registration cards from the clutter of poorly folded road maps, napkins, socket wrenches, and a box of plastic fuses.

I handed it all to the officer. He took it.

Mike and Gary and I all watched as he stared at the documents I'd passed to him, then as he lowered his sunglasses down the bridge of his sweaty nose to look at me over their thin gold frames.

He looked back again at the photo on my license, comparing the image there with the real person sitting behind the wheel of the truck.

"You need to get yourself a haircut, son," he told me. "Before school starts back up. You almost look like two different people."

"Yes, sir," I said. "I will."

That summer I had let my hair grow down past my shoulders. It was greasy and stringy from the humidity, and I knew I looked dirty and disheveled.

The officer passed me my license and insurance and registration back through the window. He hadn't even looked at the other stuff. Gary and Mike were still staring straight ahead. I could tell that they were trying not to laugh.

"Y'all have a good one," the officer said, raising his sunglasses back up the bridge of his nose and stepping away from the truck so we could go.

"Thanks," I said. "You too."

I passed the insurance and registration back to Mike, who just put them on the dashboard by the loaf of bread, and I started to ease the truck through the roadblock.

Once we had passed it, and the officers and their cars were barely visible through the back window, Gary slid the 311 from under his jeans and put it back in the tape player. I turned it as loud as it could go without busting the speakers and so that we could hear it over the wind rush coming in through the cab and the noise of the plastic bags endlessly flapping against the dash.

*

When we got back to Mike's house, I parked my truck off to the side of his yard so that it was mostly hidden by some overgrown bushes and trees. Mike's dad hoarded cars and car parts, and their yard was littered with greasy engines and rusted-out batteries and coils of hoses and stacks of busted tires. If you brushed up against them by accident, they turned your jeans black and the oil was almost impossible to get off.

Mike put the mushrooms back in the Wal-Mart bag, and we each grabbed some of the groceries and walked through the yard. Some dogs ran up to us and nuzzled at our calves and then disappeared under the shade of the sagging porch. We went inside.

No one was home, but still we went straight to Mike's room and closed the door behind us. Mike went over to the window, pulled the blinds, and clicked on the radio that was sitting on top of his scuffed dresser. A bootleg cassette of a Jane's Addiction concert leaked from the speakers and Perry Farrell's high-pitched voice crooned throughout the room as we sat down on the unmade bed and started to pop the mushrooms into our mouths, one by one, unwashed. We chased them with swigs of flat Coke.

Then, it was just a matter of waiting until they kicked in. Mike and Gary and I sat around listening to music (we had switched from Jane's Addiction to a bootleg of the new Tool album, which hadn't come out yet) and smoking cigarettes before eventually going back outside just as Maynard James Keenan was singing the opening to "Eulogy" through his slightly-distorted megaphone, Danny Carey's strange contrapuntal rhythms tapping like a steadily-dripping faucet in the background.

It was starting to get dark by then, the sky mostly gray behind the black streaks of pines stretching up overhead and casting skeletal shadows over the balding yard. I could hear a buzzing sound and the trees seemed to vibrate slightly, like plucked guitar strings.

The ground looked as though someone had tossed a giant net onto it, ready to snap us all up into the trees like in one of those old episodes of Scooby Doo that we used to watch when we were kids, sitting in one of our childhood friend's dark trailers when their parents weren't home, a loud window unit chugging in the background, everything smelling of stale cigarette smoke and beer.

But now, much older, as we walked through the woods the leaves and the mud seemed to flow and pulse like the inside of a lava lamp—one that we were inside of, too. I hadn't realized it until then that I was actually tripping.

I blinked my eyes hard against the dying light, which seemed brighter than it should have, and when I looked over at Gary and Mike, they appeared equally overwhelmed and stimulated. Gary was holding a fistful of mud and letting it ooze through his fingers and drip down his arm in long, dark rills and in the rising moonlight, it looked almost like blood. He rubbed it on his face and in his hair.

We walked through the woods for a while, not talking, getting farther and farther from Mike's house, though you could still see the warm light inside of his window glowing through the veil of dark curtains that he had draped over it. The weeds grew taller as we got deeper into the woods, and they were wet with rainwater and humidity; after a while our jeans and shoes were soaked.

None of us said anything. We just kept walking. Eventually we reached a clearing that was bathed in damp moonlight—the stars wheeling slowly overhead and limning the thick power lines stretched taut across their skeletal poles—and we stopped to sit down in the grass. Everything seemed to pulse and throb with electricity, a steadily rising hum.

"Where are we?" I finally said.

"We're in the fuckin' woods," Mike said, laughing, as he tore muddy clumps of grass from the ground. The sound of it ripping was as if he were slowly tearing the cardboard flaps off the top of a U-Haul box. I could feel it in my stomach and in my spine. I wanted to throw up but couldn't. The skin on my arms was covered with a sheen of sweat and humidity and old rainwater from the bushes and low-hanging branches we had stumbled through to get to where we were. I didn't know how long we had been walking, couldn't gauge how much time had passed since I'd eaten that handful of dirty mushrooms, but at that moment I wanted it all to be over with. I stood up, tried to steady myself against the rotating earth. The tall weeds at the perimeter of the clearing swayed and whispered.

"Can we keep going?" I said. "I'm kind of freaking out."

Gary didn't say anything, just stood, the mud on his face and arms and hair dry now and cracking like burnt paper. He had taken off his shoes and socks at some point and he was wriggling his feet in the mud and grass; it crawled up between his toes, and he seemed to sink into the earth, slowly, like he was in quicksand.

I almost sprinted from the clearing and back into the woods, tripping on branches and fallen trees, old hollowed-out logs full of cobwebs and nests of pine needles and daubs of mud and clay. The moonlight had mostly vanished behind the canopy of trees and the dark trail was less intense than being in the open, but still things buzzed at an uncomfortable sort of frequency that I didn't like anymore.

It was like being inside one of those speakers in my truck, all the bass pressing up against your body and squeezing out your organs. I could feel my legs wavering in the soft dirt and everything continued to spin: the leaves and grass humming and quivering in the thick air. I finally bent over and threw up in the mud.

When I stood back up, I felt better, more clear-headed and able to move. Mike and Gary were behind me, and their faces looked gray with sickness, but neither one of them had thrown up. I turned around and started walking deeper into the woods, sticks and dried leaves cracking underfoot as Mike and Gary followed me over what seemed to have once been a trail.

The moonlight peered through the branches overhead and occasionally lit our path as the woods began to open up and the walking became easier and more swift.

"Where are we?" Mike finally said as we stopped in another clearing.

"I don't know, but I think we went the wrong way," I said.

Gary was still quiet, looking up at the now-visible stars and moon overhead.

I squinted my eyes against the glare and could see the hulking shadows of buildings in the distance, rising up from the gloom like gigantic tombstones, whisks of fog trailing across their darkened facades like fingers tracing a line across a dusty tabletop. As my vision settled into focus, I finally knew what I was looking at.

It was our school.

We had somehow emerged from the woods just behind the football stadium, quiet and unlit during this summer evening, which seemed like the perfect spot to rest and gather ourselves for a while before heading back through the woods to Mike's house. I knew we were trespassing but figured no one would be out there to see us anyway.

I looked at Gary and Mike, who both seemed to be trying to determine whether this was some bizarre hallucination. They kept opening their eyes wide and then shutting them, as if that would shake the image away from their vision if it wasn't really there. But every time they looked ahead, their faces became less confused and more accepting of this suddenly new reality.

"Y'all want to go over there?" I said.

Gary looked at me, then back toward the stadium. He smiled, and for what seemed like the first time that night, he finally said something. "Yeah."

I looked over at Mike, who just nodded.

"Well, let's go then," I said.

*

If you had been standing atop the cement bleachers of the stadium that evening, looking out over the dark woods, the trees glistening under the moonlight, maybe you would have seen three small silhouettes emerging into the gravel lot, punctuated by the tiny orange glow of their cigarettes dangling at their sides. Maybe you would have wondered who they were, where they were coming from, why they were there.

You would have seen them walk over the gravel, limned white and spackled with shadows from the light poles that stood unlit in the parking lot. You may have even heard the rocks crunching under their shoes— or beneath Gary's bare feet. You would have seen them disappear under the bleachers momentarily as they made their way onto the damp football field and then stretched out on the soft grass, washed in moonlight. Sprawling their arms and legs about as if they were making snow angels out there.

Then, after a while, you would have seen them get up and make their way to the edge of the field, whose perimeter was closed off with an eight-foot-high chain-link fence. You would hear it clink and stretch as they climbed over it, one by one, then disappear down a gravel road toward the school itself, then to wherever it was they lived or came from.

You might start to wonder what became of them after that—if you had really seen those three figures at all, or if it was just some story your imagination created to deal with the lonely feeling of standing atop a football stadium. Alone. In the dark. On the Fourth of July.

But, even if they had been real, you wouldn't have seen them as they walked alongside the highway later that evening and a police cruiser stopped and pulled over behind them, its blue lights flashing over their damp and sallow-looking faces before two officers finally emerged and patted them down against the hood, taking their lighters and cigarettes, a small pocketknife.

"Didn't we see you boys earlier today?" one of the officers would say. "At the traffic stop in Goodbee?"

"No, sir," one of the boys would lie, though you would be able to tell he recognized the officer, who was now nudging all three of them into the back seat with his baton.

You wouldn't have heard as the car pulled off from the gravel shoulder and one of the officers turned on the radio and Twisted Sister's "We're Not Gonna Take It" blared from the speakers inside the car and the boys, all three of them, tried as hard as they could not to laugh at this new strange circumstance in which they found themselves. They were still tripping, after all, and this just added to the surreal nature of the situation.

There also would have been no way for you to see the police cruiser as it took the boys straight back to Mike's house, maneuvering between the stacks of tires and car parts in the driveway before stopping in front of the porch, several curious dogs emerging from underneath the soggy slats and barking through the wash of headlights, a yellow lamp coming on from inside the den, the boys climbing from the back seat and into the yard, still shocked they hadn't been arrested, the metal cuffs clicking over their wrists before being taken to the St. Tammany Parish Jail.

Instead, they went inside and back to Mike's room—his parents never said a word to them as they walked down the narrow hall—where they sat on Mike's bed and put the stereo on low, something mellow like Pink Floyd to bring them down as they marveled at the events of the evening and their dumb, idiot luck.

And you wouldn't have seen them a couple of weeks later, when they did this again: picking mushrooms from a cow field out in the country, then eating them and driving around in the dark, trying their luck again. Eventually, they'd end up at the movie theater, where they'd buy tickets to see *Independence*

Day, the movie about an alien invasion, and how one of them would start to think everything happening on the screen was real, and he would get up and run to the bathroom, puke, then stare at his face in the mirror, his skin pale and green-hued under the fluorescent lighting.

You wouldn't be able to see him leave and go out to his truck, sit there by himself for two hours until the movie finished and his friends came out—you wouldn't know the thoughts he had and how he'd imagined he had died out there in the sweaty cab of that truck, parked on the side of the movie theater in a ditch, how everything seemed to bob and float as if he were on top of a body of water.

And you wouldn't have seen the other moviegoers who had come out and laughed at him as he smoked cigarette after cigarette under the swarm of moths bathing in the overhead security light, his window rolled down, his sweat-gleaned and quivering arm dangling at the side of the truck like a windless flag. Waiting for his friends to come back, waiting for it to all be over with.

But even if you had heard and seen these things from up there, you wouldn't have ever believed them in the first place, would you?

Mirrors

My wife and kids and I have just gotten home from spending the afternoon at the St. Tammany Parish Fair in Covington, Louisiana. I sit down at my computer with a cup of coffee and open my email. I'm tired, and I still have work to do, but I'm glad I've been able to do something fun with my family today.

I've been going to this same fair ever since I was a kid. And not much about it has changed in these thirty-odd years either. There's still the Gravitron, a saucer-shaped ride that spins and creates a powerful centrifugal force with its movement, causing its riders to stick to the plastic pads that line its curved walls like a bunch of mattresses leaning on the inside of a furniture store. People maneuver themselves against the generated pressure in order to turn their bodies horizontally, diagonally, or even head-down as the ride spins and spins around its creaking axis, pressing them against the wall. At least this is what I've been told. I've never actually ridden it myself.

I'm not much for rides or carnivals or fairs. I never really was. But I went to them as a kid, and so now I go out of a sense of nostalgia, a desperate sort of longing for my past, and maybe even for the spectacle of it, if I'm being completely honest. But most importantly, I go for my kids. I go so they can have their own set of memories and stories to tell one day. It's one of the most important things I can think of to give them.

My favorite part of going to the fair when I was younger was walking down the midway at night: the smells of food being fried, cotton candy, cigarette smoke, sweat, dust, hay, and grass, all mingling together into one, a conglomeration of smells—along with the sounds of people screaming and laughing as the rides whorled and creaked on their rusty tracks and around their axes; country music playing from cheap radios hanging from bungee cords behind the prize booths; horses, chickens, and sheep making their own noises from the livestock barns in the distance.

I would step over the orange and black extension cords that snaked across the dusty patches of grass and disappeared under idling RVs or semi-trailers, or beneath the myriad wooden booths where you could win prizes for knocking over metal milk jugs with a baseball or tossing rings around the neck of a rubber duck bobbing in a plastic pool filled with murky gray water. You could throw a dart to pop half-inflated balloons tacked to a corkboard behind some leather-skinned dude holding a cigarette between his lips, or you could use a water pistol to knock over a taunting, tiny metal clown—something ominous and almost threatening in his painted grin and cheeks as the water cascades down them like tears and then lands in a steel trough below where it's collected and then siphoned back into the long rubber hoses for the water guns.

The prizes you got were never much, never near what you spent to get them, but one year I remember I was lucky enough to win a pocketknife. It had a wooden handle and a blade that folded out, and my stepdad even carved my initials into it with a wood-burning tool, its metal tip bright orange with heat as he tattooed the letters DA onto the soft, tan wood.

Another year, I won a small glass plaque with the cover of Mötley Crüe's latest album, *Dr. Feelgood*, embossed on its smudged and shiny surface. I kept it in my room in the trailer where I grew up, on the thin wall next to pictures I had cut out from *Mad* magazine or the comics section in the Sunday *Times-Picayune*.

I remember my stepdad would usually drink as we walked around those crowded fairgrounds, his hand gripping a can of Budweiser wrapped in a damp, brown paper bag. This would usually put him in a good, often generous mood. He would buy my stepbrother, stepsister, and me all caramel corn and Barq's root beer in glass bottles and let us ride the bumper cars or get tickets to walk through the fun house, its maze of mirrors bending and distorting your image so that you hardly recognized yourself in that strange and smoky darkness.

Once he even convinced me to get on the Scrambler with my stepsister, even though I hated rides and was scared of all the things I imagined going wrong on them: a loose screw, a broken chain, people getting maimed as a result of these mechanical imperfections. Even before I read about things like this actually happening, my imagination would conjure horrors such as razor blades being stuck in the cracks of the seats, just waiting for someone to slide over them as they eased themselves into the ride. But despite this, and since I was even more afraid of my stepdad thinking I was a coward, I climbed into the sticky silver car next to my stepsister as she pulled the metal safety bar over our legs, and we waited for the ride to start.

It spun us backward and sideways, it jerked left and right and up and down as we were tossed around like a handful of gravel in a clothes dryer. It was awful. The last thing I remember before throwing up all over my tennis shoes—as well as my stepsister's and on the people sitting next to us—was the line of spectators on the other side of the steel barricades surrounding the ride, watching us spin and whorl, their faces becoming distorted and blurry as we circled erratically like I was back inside that fun house, unsure of what was real and what wasn't.

I never rode on a ride like that again.

And so, I'm thinking about all these things after having spent the afternoon at the fair with my own family, as I come inside now and sit down at the computer to check my email. How much my life has changed since then, back when I was just a kid at the fair with my stepdad and stepsiblings, most of them gone from my life now for one reason or another, and me with my own kids, my own life carved out in this world.

It's hard not to mull over your past. Especially because today, when I open my email, I discover that I've been sent the results from a DNA paternity test that I had taken last month, one that will hopefully determine after all these years, and without any more doubt, who my biological father is.

*

Maybe I should have begun all of this by saying that for my whole life, I thought I knew who my biological father was, even though I had been adopted, and it wasn't until I was in my late thirties and took a DNA test that I learned what I had believed for so long to be true was, in fact, not. But beginnings are difficult, and so are endings. So, people often start their stories in the middle, from some liminal place like that fun house at the parish fair, all those mirrors and twisted walls disorienting you and making it hard to find your way out.

So, let me try it this way: I sip from my coffee, watch for a minute the steam as it wisps from my cup, then I lean forward and click open the message, download the PDF attachment, and slowly start to read that there is a greater than 99.99 percent probability that a man whom I've never met, who lives over a thousand miles away from me and in a city and state where I've never been—and, until just recently, has a name I've never heard before in my entire life—is my father.

My hands are shaking so badly that I take them away from the keyboard and stare at the screen, reading the same words over and over again, as though maybe I've missed something in the way they are written.

*

And here's yet another way I could have started this:

My mother wasn't married when I was born, and so in the space on my birth certificate where it had the word "FATHER," the letters "N/A" were typed beneath it. But my mother had told her family who she *believed* my father was, and everyone just accepted that as the truth. His name was Lonnie, she had told them. She had known him since they were kids. Lonnie's father was friends with my grandfather. And even though my mother was somewhat promiscuous around the time I was conceived, no one in my family ever questioned my paternal roots—at least not that I know of. They later passed that information on to me as I grew up and started asking about where I came from. I had no real reason to question it either.

But I've written about this before in another memoir: my mother's schizophrenia, her inability to take care of me, my adoption, my search for Lonnie, the man who I had always been told was my father. I have written about finding and eventually meeting him when I was in my late twenties, just before my own kids were born. I have also written about the disappointment I felt, the emptiness, but also about the hope I found in becoming a father myself, and about what I thought of as my chance to absolve my children from what I saw as Lonnie's dark past.

But what I haven't written about yet is that this man Lonnie, who I had believed my whole life was my father, was actually not related to me at all.

I had met him and had visited him at his house on several occasions. I had brought my wife and kids along with me a couple of those times. I had talked with him on the phone and via email before eventually losing touch with him altogether. I even met his family several years after that, when one of his sisters found out about me on Facebook and invited me to a reunion; I took pictures with all of them. Hugged them, kissed them, and loved them like the relatives I thought they were. I cried with them about what we had all thought was a shared connection, a lost past.

I wrote stories and poems about Lonnie—a whole novel, as a matter of fact—as I tried for most of my adult life to assimilate my biological connection to him (and all the implications of that connection) into my existence. I kept pictures of him in a red Wolverine boot box on the top shelf of my closet, right along with all the other family pictures I keep there. I had felt sadness and guilt when I learned of his death from throat cancer, remorse that I hadn't even found out until many months after it happened. I had spent a lot of time thinking about his alcoholism, his depression, his loneliness, and what those things meant for me as a man and as a father. And all of this to ultimately learn that he had no biological connection to me whatsoever. It's the kind of thing that changes your life in ways you can't number, the kind of thing that makes you question who you are and who you've always been.

Should I have been angry at my mother for this? For not even knowing the man who fathered me, her only child, her only son? Or did she know but didn't want to tell me? Was she trying to protect me from something? But as all these questions were forming in my mind, my mother passed away. I would never get the chance to ask her these things. I still wonder if she died with a different truth in her mind, one that she just couldn't bring herself to share. But like so many other things in my life, I'll never have that answer.

Now I have a new answer, though, sitting here in front of my computer screen, my hands still shaking. I somehow manage to forward the email to the man who I now know is my father. I don't tell him what the results are in the message, just that they are attached—in case he doesn't want to know right away, in case he wants time to think about the implications of the results before he opens them: that he has a son, a thirty-eight-year-old man with a wife and two children, a person whom he has never laid eyes on until recently—and even then, only through pictures posted on Facebook. A person he had never known about until he received a text message one Saturday morning just two months ago, asking if he ever knew a woman with my mother's name or if he was, by any chance, in Louisiana during the late 1970s when I would have been conceived.

*

Still, maybe even after all these things I've just said, this story really starts here:

It was early summer, and I was getting ready to go to a meeting for work. On a whim, I logged in to Ancestry.com to view my DNA matches from a test I had taken and sent in a couple of years earlier. A friend had bought the kit for me after he had read one of my novels and I told him the story about Lonnie—that the book was based on my meeting him. This friend told me that he had actually worked for Lonnie's father years before, and so he took great interest in my history.

Anyway, every so often, a new distant cousin would pop up or maybe some other family member I hadn't thought about in a while. Interestingly, nothing there ever connected me to Lonnie, but I wrote it off. It was possible that none of his relatives had ever taken the test. I never thought to even question that. It was all just for fun at that point.

I had mostly lost interest in the site by then, anyway, after having never gleaned anything new about my family or my ancestry to keep me going back to it. But for some reason, I logged in on that particular morning. I don't know why. It was just something to look at until I had to leave for work.

As I clicked my name to pull up my DNA matches, I noticed a new result, right beneath a first cousin on my maternal side. It was a name I had never seen before, had never even heard of. The shared DNA indicated that this person was either another first cousin or perhaps a half-uncle. I knew that my mother's sisters or brother hadn't had any other children—not to mention the fact that I didn't share this connection with my maternal cousin anyway—so the only possibility I could determine was that one of Lonnie's sisters had a child whom I hadn't heard of before. I Googled the name and found someone a little bit older than me who lived about two hours away. He had brown hair, blue eyes. It was a cousin. Had to be.

I mentioned all of this to my wife as I was walking out the door. "That's weird," was all she said. I agreed that it was. Then, I left for work.

During breaks in the meeting, I used my laptop to find out more information about this new relative. Fortunately, there was a lot online, but I still wasn't sure who he was, or exactly how we were connected. I texted a picture of him to my wife.

"Lol. You're crazy," she texted back.

Maybe I was. Most likely this was all just a mistake. After all, the friend who had ordered the DNA kit for me was letting me use his account on Ancestry, so maybe our results had gotten mixed up somehow. I emailed him to ask if he had heard of this person, if he had any relatives with that last name.

"No," he told me.

Now I couldn't stop thinking about this person. I messaged some people on Lonnie's side of the family, people whom I had just recently met, and asked them if one of Lonnie's sisters—or if their grandfather—had any children no one knew about.

"No," they all said. "That would be impossible."

"But, then again," one of them said, "we didn't know about you until recently, so I guess it's not completely out of the question. Keep us updated."

I told them I would.

Coincidentally, one of Lonnie's sisters had recently taken the DNA test on Ancestry too, but as far as I knew, she was still waiting for her results to come back. Before this, I had no doubt that it would link me to her as a nephew. Now, I was starting to wonder if it actually would. There were still a lot of possibilities, and I was already drowning in information and potential outcomes. It was maddening, to say the least.

I kept searching names and pictures for the rest of the day until I got home. Finally, I messaged the person directly through Ancestry's email service. He responded but was just as confused by this possible connection as I was. Thankfully, like me, he at least seemed curious to find out more. But after that first contact, we lost touch altogether. I'm not sure why. I wondered if he had found out something he didn't want to tell me.

*

During this time, my mother was in hospice care, dying of cancer. I hadn't spoken to her in several years, but after receiving a text a couple of days before my birthday earlier that year, informing me about her illness, I went with my wife and children to visit her at a hospital in Meridian, Mississippi.

When we were on our way there, I got another text saying that my mother found out I was coming and wanted me to bring her two fish sandwiches from McDonald's. So, when we got to Meridian, I pulled into the drive-thru to get them for her. It was as though no time had passed at all between us in the years since I'd last spoken to her. Still, I was terrified about how she would react when she saw me, heard my voice. I had written a memoir about my life with her and could only hope she hadn't seen it. She would have been mortified by its existence if she had.

But, when my family and I walked into the room that morning, my mother just looked up at me and smiled. *Roseanne* was playing on the little TV hanging from the wall, the sound low.

"Hey, David," was all she said. "I guess you heard I'm dying, huh?"

"Yeah, Susie. I heard. Are you feeling all right?"

"Yeah," she said. "For now." Then she pointed at the McDonald's bag in my hand. "Thanks for getting those. Is that the fish sandwiches?"

"Yeah," I told her.

"Good. Thank you, David. You can just put it on the table over there if you want. The food's terrible in this place, man."

Nothing had changed. It really was as though I had just seen her the day before.

My wife and kids and I spent several hours with my mother that day. At some point, I reminded her that it was my birthday. I don't know why. I just wanted to tell her that.

"Yeah, I know that, David," she said. "Thirty-eight years old. Damn. That's somethin'. You better take care of yourself, so you don't end up like me."

Then, she said that she wanted me to take a picture with her. "This might be the last one you ever get," she said. "I'm finished, man." I'll never forget how she said it like that.

Anyway, despite a grim prognosis, my mother lived another six months, and I found myself suddenly thrust back into her life. I kept in touch with her as much as I could, making the drive to where she eventually ended up—a nursing home in Diamondhead, Mississippi, right down the road from where one of Lonnie's sisters lived. I told my mother about that coincidence—one in a series of many others that were starting to happen then. This was even before I had discovered anything on Ancestry, though. At that time, I still thought Lonnie was my father. I had had no reason not to.

My mother would just say, "Don't worry about Lonnie. He was a dead-beat. I should've picked a different father for you." She said this as though it were that easy. Maybe it was. I don't know.

But now I wonder if she knew, even then, that Lonnie wasn't my father. Had she been trying to tell me that in her own bizarre way?

In the past, depending on her mood, my mother would mention names of other people she thought might have been my father. She mentioned a musician once. Someone she met in a bar, I think. Until then, I never knew there was any question in her mind about it. I just thought she was trying to make me feel better about Lonnie. I still don't know what she was thinking when she told me those things.

I spent my mother's birthday with her that year, on what would turn out to be her last. I brought her a slice of cheesecake from Rouse's and a card and a potted plant for her room at the nursing home, where hospice would come to care for her. She had some sort of catheter in her back, draining fluid from her kidneys, and she was in a lot of pain. I remember she kept a picture of me and my family tacked onto a corkboard in her room, the image of my face completely rubbed out from her thumb constantly going over it again and again. She did things like that.

On one visit not long after her birthday, just when I discovered this new match on Ancestry, I asked my mother if she had ever heard of this person who was suddenly showing up as my first cousin or half-uncle. She leaned against the bed from where she had been sitting in a wheelchair, hunched over in pain, then looked at the wall as she seemed to think about what I had just asked her.

After a good twenty seconds, she just said, "No, David. Lonnie's your father."

I never brought it up again. And when I finally did learn that what she told me wasn't true, it was too late. She had finally succumbed to her illness after six long and painful months.

*

Before I took the official paternity test with the man who I would ultimately discover is my father, I spent countless hours online that summer researching newspaper archives, census records, obituaries, marriage licenses, military documents, high school yearbooks, basically anything that was in the public domain that might help me find out who this man was. It was all I could do.

Based on the Ancestry connection I had learned about, I was able to narrow the possibilities down a good bit, but still hadn't discovered anything conclusive yet. I would look at pictures from Facebook profiles and compare them to pictures of myself. When I saw my reflection in the mirror, I would notice features I hadn't seen before, things I had attributed all these years to my mother, since, save for my fair skin and blue eyes, I shared very little resemblance with Lonnie.

Now, I noticed the curve of my mouth, the color of my lips, the creases at the corners of my eyes. I saw all these features in a different way, as part of a genetic pool I hadn't known existed before. I would see pictures online of people I now knew were my relatives and notice those same features on them. But these people were all from a different part of the country, places I've never even been, so I went back and forth between thinking this was all still just some crazy mistake to wondering what my mother had been hiding from everyone all these years, and why.

Around this same time, Lonnie's sister finally received her own DNA test results on Ancestry. They indicated that we shared no biological connection, meaning that there was no possible way Lonnie was my father. My life was changing very quickly, like I was back on the Scrambler at the parish fair as a kid. I just had to keep holding on as best I could.

And now, in addition to everything else, I started to feel guilty about Lonnie's family, who had all just recently accepted me as one of their own. I worried that they might think I had been lying to them to get attention. I also wondered what Lonnie would think, if he were still alive—that he had invested spending his time and emotional energy on me, only to discover that he wasn't my father after all. I even remember him expressing his doubts to me once—on the day my son was born, of all times—asking if I'd be willing to take a DNA test, but I had been so offended that he had even asked me that, and by the *way* he had asked it, that I never agreed to do it. I was *that* convinced he was my father, that what my mother had said all those years was true. Now I wonder how differently my life would have unfolded had I taken that test back then in 2008, when he was still alive. The thought of it keeps me awake at night.

Around this time, I started watching a show on TLC called *Long Lost Family*, in which parents are reunited with their children after many years. Sometimes the child never knew they were adopted until they came across a birth certificate by mistake, wandering around in an attic or a basement one day, looking through old boxes of photographs and newspapers, throwing their entire existence into question. I could relate. I would lay in bed and sob when the adult children on the show were reunited with their parents—the often-instant connection they had, how much they looked alike sometimes, how similar their interests were.

There was one episode I remember in which a woman had been looking for her father and, like me, had run into roadblock after roadblock in her unsuccessful search. All she had was a first name. Her mother had told her that she was a product of a one-night stand and that she had met the girl's father in a pizza parlor in Seattle where she had worked as a waitress. The man in question never even knew he had a child.

But when they were finally connected after the daughter's long-drawn-out efforts to find him, they not only looked alike, but both had the same careers working with animal sanctuaries in Oregon. I still cry when I think about that, and I hoped that I could possibly have a connection like that with my own father one day. But I would have to find out who he was first.

*

A few days after my mother died, my wife and kids and I drove to Gulfport, Mississippi, to pick up her ashes. We were gone all day, I remember, having stopped first at the nursing home in Diamondhead where she had spent her last days in hospice care. We picked up her belongings, which had been placed in several large, black plastic yard bags, put them in our trunk, then headed down the interstate toward Gulfport.

At some point, we almost had to pull over when two large dogs that had apparently fallen out from the bed of a pickup truck, and which had been since mutilated by passing cars and semis, were lying in the middle of the road, getting hit again and again by speeding vehicles—some of the cars swerving off onto the shoulder, running over the sleeper lines and causing the air around us to rumble as if a cluster of jets was flying overhead. I looked back in the rearview mirror to see the poor dogs' bodies tumbling around on the asphalt like the yard bags we had in our trunk. They were bloody and torn and mangled. I checked to make sure my children hadn't seen them, but they both were looking peacefully at their phones—one of the rare moments when I was happy for those electronic distractions.

After that, when we finally got to Gulfport, almost the entire downtown area was blocked off in places, the roads torn apart, PVC pipes stacked on the side of the street, orange-and-white barricades keeping us from getting to the funeral home where my mother's ashes were. Construction workers directed us down a circuitous path that just kept putting us in the same place where we had started. It was like something out of *As I Lay Dying*.

Eventually, I just parked our car and we all walked to the funeral home, which was an old house with creaky floors and musty furniture. The lady who greeted us at the door knew who I was as soon as we got inside; I guess because of the resemblance between my face and that of my mother's in the picture I had sent them the day before, which was her high school senior picture. It was the most beautiful picture of her I had, and as weird as it might sound—especially to someone who was actually raised by their mother—I used to keep it in my wallet when I was a kid, take it out and look at it sometimes when I missed her, which happened often in my life growing up.

The lady went into a room toward the back of the house, the floor creaking under her high heels as she walked away, then came back and handed me a wooden box with my mother's name on it. She explained to me how the bodies were cremated and the measures they took to ensure that the remains belonged to the person whose name was listed on the box. Then, she told me about some of the options for how to preserve the ashes: there were glass-blown pendants, she said, in which your loved one's remains could be blown directly into the glass and then you could wear it around your neck; they also offered fancy urns and other types of jewelry. I just listened to her as she handed me a catalog, placing it atop the wooden box that held my mother's ashes.

After we left the funeral home, the traffic was so bad that we decided to stop at the beach. We rolled up our pants and walked through the warm, shallow brown water of the Gulf of Mexico, the oil platforms in the hazy distance like the skeletons of so many time-ravaged buildings in some city that had been flooded and destroyed. We walked through the water, finding seashells and animal bones and glass bottles as a cluster of Blue Angels F/A-18 Hornets flew overhead, thundering the sky around us. Some people passing by told us that the jets were practicing for an air show that weekend.

"Are y'all going?" they asked.

"No, we're just passing through," I told them.

"Well, that might be for the best," they said, looking up at the graying sky and the vee of jets cutting a path through the dark clouds above us. "Looks like we're in for some pretty bad weather this afternoon."

Almost as soon as they said it, the sky seemed to unload itself. The rain came down hard and in big, heavy drops. It pocked the sand as though someone were dropping marbles from the roof of a skyscraper. My wife and kids and I ran back to the car, nearly covered in water and wet, sticky sand.

It rained the whole way back, a line of dark clouds coming right toward us from the west. Still, we stopped at my mother's house in Waveland to check on her property before we went home. It was the first time I had been there in years, since I left my mother standing in the overgrown yard one afternoon, never to speak to her again for a long, long time.

But the house had been broken into, the door torn from its frame, everything my mother kept inside tossed around on the floor and counters of her dirty kitchen as though a strong storm had blown through. Since my mother was a severe hoarder, it was hard to tell what was trash and what wasn't. There were at least twenty or thirty empty boxes of Honey-Nut Cheerios on the ground outside, some of them damp and sun-bleached, trails of ants crawling out from their bent lids.

Seeing these things brought back too many painful memories of my mother's illness, not to mention my being afraid that whoever had broken in and vandalized the place might still be there, or otherwise be on their way back. I thought about calling the police, but I knew that any chance of saving what was left here was gone now anyway. So, we left.

When we finally got home later that evening, there was a letter in the mail from a woman who said she had been friends with my mother when they were kids, that they had stayed in touch into early adulthood, just as my mother's illness became too great for her to deal with. She told me how gifted my mother had always been, but that she had so much trouble functioning in day-to-day life. Of course, I knew these things, but it was nice to hear them from someone else.

She also said she had remembered meeting me once when I was a baby, when my mother still had custody of me, and that even though they had lost touch over the years, she had followed the progress of my life and had hoped I would receive her note in the spirit with which it was intended: being that of someone who had concern for me and my family and our well-being.

I didn't think it would have been possible to cry any more than I had in the past six months—learning of my mother's sickness, watching her die slowly and in pain, being uprooted by this new mystery surrounding the identity of my biological father—but as I tried to read the note aloud to my wife that late afternoon, I finally just had to hand it over to her so she could read it herself. I couldn't do it anymore. I was completely choked up.

Part of me felt as though my mother was still communicating with me in some strange way. All the odd occurrences on the trip to get her ashes, then coming home to find this letter. What was she trying to tell me, though? The morning I got the call saying that my mother had passed, I remember I opened the blinds to my bedroom window and saw a large butterfly just sitting there on a tiny branch, its wing lightly wisping against the glass. I swear it sat there for a full minute. I stared at it, took in its myriad colors, its slow and peaceful movements. There was something reassuring about its presence, as though my mother was saying she was finally all right.

I believed her.

When my wife was finished reading the letter, I responded to it via email, thanking this woman for her sympathies about my mother and mentioning to her my recent search for my father. I asked her if she knew anyone my mother might have dated around the time I was conceived.

She wrote me back and said that she didn't know too many of the men my mother was involved with, but she did remember my mother living with a man whom she had met while staying at River Oaks, the psychiatric hospital she had been committed to after her first husband left her. *Could that person have been my father?* I wondered. It almost made a strange sort of sense. But it still wasn't the definitive answer I was looking for.

My mother's friend also told me that she had known Lonnie, and that when she asked him about me once in the early 1980s, he denied having anything to do with my existence. She hadn't wanted to mention that to me, she said, but since I brought it up, she told me that she had always doubted Lonnie's being my father as well. There was just so much new information coming at me all at once, I hardly knew how I would process it. Or if I ever would be able to.

*

After several months of searching online and contacting as many people as I could find, the man who I would later find out is my biological father called me on the phone. It was a Friday afternoon, and I was in the carpool line with my wife, picking up our kids from school. I had already saved his number in my phone from the time several weeks earlier when I had sent him a text message asking if he knew my mother, so I knew who it was as soon as the phone started ringing. I showed the phone to my wife, the name blinking on its screen, then let it go to voice mail. There were strict rules prohibiting cell phone use in the carpool line, not to mention how nervous I was. Why was he calling me? What would we say?

We hadn't taken the paternity test yet, though he had already agreed to via email. Had he called to tell me he had changed his mind? Had he remembered some detail about my mother that I would want to know?

When we got home, I returned his call. I tried not to think too much about how the conversation would go. I just dialed his number. He answered on the second or third ring, and I heard his voice for the first time uttering my name, this man who would one day turn out to be my father. As we talked, I paced around outside in our driveway and in the one-lane road fronting our house. The asphalt was warm against my bare feet. It was September 14, 2018.

We talked for about fifteen minutes, and I was happy to hear that this man sounded kind, sensitive, intelligent. He sounded like the kind of person anyone would want for a father. He shared with me a little bit about his own life, then we discussed the specifics of how we would proceed with the paternity test. We would both receive a swab in the mail, follow the instructions for collecting our respective samples, and send them back in to be processed. Then, we'd both wait for the results.

*

I mentioned before that beginnings and endings are hard, and I think I meant that to be about life as well as about writing stories. If I'm being completely honest, I'll say that I don't really know how to end this, just like I wasn't sure about where to start. It's like I'm standing in that fun house all over again, a child trying to find his way around in a maze of darkness and mirrors.

So, I'll end it this way, even though this is really just another beginning:

In less than two weeks from now, as I sit here writing all of this in a journal that my father sent to me this past Christmas, I will meet him in person for the first time in my life—he'll fly in the day before my thirty-ninth birthday, almost one year to the day after I received a text message telling me that my mother was dying from cancer. He and I will spend my birthday together, at my house. He will meet my kids, his grandchildren.

I like to think of all this as my mother's last gift to me, especially since, after she died, I would ask her every day to help me find out who my father was. Maybe she really didn't know the answer when she was alive, and maybe she would have been embarrassed if she had known it wasn't Lonnie, the man whom she had insisted it had been all those years. I will never know the answer to that.

But after communicating with my father these past couple of months— ever since we received the paternity results the day I got home from the fair that day, talking via Skype and email and on the phone, learning about him and his life, looking at pictures of him (we look almost identical at certain stages of our lives)—I am grateful he and my mother met, however briefly that may have been. All I can say is that I'm here as a result of that meeting. And that now there's a sense of a new life being breathed into mine, not incredibly different or any less magical than when my own two children were born.

Or maybe this is a better place to end:

When I was a kid, we used to go this place called The Pizza Man in Covington, right across from the fairgrounds I mentioned earlier. Each October, you could see the rides from the parking lot, lit up and spinning in the night sky. You could even hear all the sounds from it across the street.

The Pizza Man was one of about three restaurants where you could eat back then, and so we went there all the time. After we ate, we would all walk around the corner to Video Co-Op, a movie rental store where we rented VHS tapes and Nintendo games.

And we always had a good time, too. My stepdad would drink beer, the jukebox would play old songs from the sixties and seventies: Peter, Paul, and Mary, Bob Dylan, The Mamas & the Papas. As you waited for your food, you could watch the guy flipping pizza dough into saucers through the finger-printed glass that looked into the kitchen.

I still go there on my birthday almost every year when I can, even though my stepdad's dead now and everyone else has all gone their own way—married, moved, etc. But like so much else in my life, this place hasn't really changed at all in thirty years. They still have the same folded paper menu, the same songs on the jukebox, skein of flour on the floor, the same pictures on the wall: pizza boxes with funny drawings on the covers, framed puzzles of the Sistine Chapel and the Last Supper, all under the same dim lighting.

But lately, I go with my wife and my own two kids. Just to remember the good things about my life—like when we all go to the fair each year—to share these things with my family so they'll hopefully have something good, like I do, to remember one day.

And it always hits me right in the gut, the memory of it all, like a different life I'm watching on TV. But nothing like this: last week we went there, sort of on a whim, and I took my son to the bathroom after we had all finished eating. My wife and daughter stayed at the table, watching the pizza man flip pizzas behind the glass window looking into the kitchen, "California Dreamin'" playing on the jukebox.

I was already full of nostalgia and longing, so when I saw my son looking in the mirror while he was washing his hands, it occurred to me that I had probably looked in that exact same mirror thirty years ago—that's how little this place had changed since then. And I would have likely been just about the age he is now. Suddenly, his face started becoming my face, his hands my hands. He was becoming *me*. And maybe, in turn, becoming my father, whose face I see now every single time I look in the mirror.

It's a simple thing most people probably take for granted—who they resemble, where their features come from. They see it when they look in a mirror or at pictures of themselves. I thought about that fun house again. How the mirrors in there are curved and refract light in such a way that you can hardly recognize yourself in their warped perimeters.

But now I'm watching my own son look into a mirror, one through which he can see himself clearly, can know who he is, will hopefully never have to question that fact like I've had to do. Then, I thought about how incredible it is when things barrel at you like that. Unexpectedly. Like a gift. When time folds in on itself so that your past meets the present in one fluid motion. Like the ends of a sheet of paper—or like one of those folding pictures from *Mad* magazine like I used to tack onto my wall as a kid—the ones that when you bend them in such a way, what once seemed muddled now reveals something entirely new and surprising.

Coda
Family Album

First Picture: *My father, from his high school yearbook, 1964*

I found this photograph in an online archive when searching for my biological father several years ago. Until then, I didn't know who he was, had never seen him before, had never even heard his name in conversation. But here he is, in a group photograph for the Hi-Y Club; he's standing on the far right, taller than all the other boys at just over six feet. His head is tilted to the side, he's wearing a black sweater, and he's smiling jovially. When I show the picture to my wife—speechless and quivering as I point at the computer screen after so many long months of searching—she squints and says, "Wait, is that *you?*"

Second Picture: *My mother, holding me in her lap, 1982*

I'm two years old, and in this picture, my mother looks as if she just woke up, though it's likely early afternoon and I've been awake since morning. She does that sometimes. Or otherwise, she might leave altogether, not telling anyone where she is for days or weeks at a time. Anyway, we're sitting in the kitchen, and my mother is still in her nightgown. I'm dressed in a little pair of jeans and a striped shirt with buttons on it, and my shoes are on but already coming untied. We both have the same thick, wavy hair, feathering down over our ears and covering the backs of our necks. My grandmother must have fed me breakfast that morning. But she's getting tired of taking care of me, of my mother's inconsistent behavior. Not too long from now, my mother will have to give me up for adoption. And I won't see her again for almost twenty years.

Third Picture: *My father, standing outside, smiling, circa 1965*

He would have been about seventeen or so in this picture, and when I look at it, I have to catch myself and remember to breathe. It's startling how much we look alike; we could almost be the same person. He has his head tilted to the side again, like I do in pictures, self-conscious of our height, but he's still smiling—the same half-smile as mine. He's wearing a windbreaker and is standing in front of a building whose partially visible sign appears to contain the word "geology." You can make out what looks like the word "institute" just above that. Is he there on a school field trip maybe? Or a special class assignment? Was it a family vacation? I don't know, but I find myself creating these stories about him to give my own life meaning, to make sense of who I am, where I came from. It's all I can do at this point.

I received this photograph not long after a paternity test confirmed my father's and my biological connection, though my mother hadn't ever mentioned him to me before. In fact, she had told everyone, including me, that another man was my father. And I had met that man, hugged him, spent time with him in his home, took my wife and kids there so they could meet him, too. I had even written a novel about him, imagining what his life had been like, what made him who he was and, as a result, me who I am.

And even though we looked nothing alike and had very little in common, why wouldn't I have believed what my mother and everyone else told me so many times?

Fourth Picture: *My mother, Fort Walton Beach, 1966*
The glare from the sun is making her squint at the camera but you can see her hair blowing in the gulf breeze. She's wearing a light blue shirt, buttoned up the front, the long white stretch of beach behind her. Even then, she had already started to exhibit signs of mental illness, and she would soon be hospitalized, receive electroshock therapy, though none of that would do much good.

She had trouble in school, trouble at home, but she was incredibly gifted. Her parents sent her off to college to study art. She designed a few ads for local businesses, but then they asked her to leave, called my grandfather at work and told him to come pick her up. So, he did.

He got her an apartment in New Orleans, helped her with a job. She worked at Werlein's Music in the French Quarter for a while. (She was an incredibly gifted pianist, could play *Clair de Lune* from memory, even after not sitting in front of a keyboard for twenty years. And you could tell she really *felt* each note, what they all meant on a deep, emotional level.)

Then, my mother started using drugs; she was promiscuous, and by the time I was conceived in the late 1970s, it was anyone's guess who my father could have been.

Fifth Picture: *My father, sitting, 1970s*

He's wearing a light blue leisure suit, leather shoes, and he's lounging in some sort of wicker canopy chair. His hair is long and thick, like mine, and you can see him smiling beneath his full mustache, the way it makes his eyes squint at the camera. He looks happy.

And although this picture was taken in a part of the country where my mother had never even been before—the place near where my father was born and raised, and where almost everyone in his family still lives—it starts to make sense when I learn that his job in sales took him all over America, as far as Houston, Texas, even, where he lived for a while in the late '70s and drove every so often to New Orleans for an occasional long weekend in the French Quarter. He loved music and art and good food, books. And he still does. Just like me.

Sixth Picture: *My mother and me, in the hospital, 2018*

It's my thirty-eighth birthday, and I haven't seen my mother in five years. But I get a call saying that she is sick, really sick, and so I take my wife and kids up to Meridian, Mississippi, to visit her in the hospital.

And it's like no time has passed between us, just like the first day we met, when I was twenty. I remember that she had put her hands on my face, feeling all the contours and lines of my nose, my chin, my mouth, my ears, and eyes. I let her do it, too. She later told me that she had nightmares all her life that someone was pulling me from her arms, and even though she screamed and cried and begged them to let me go, she would always wake up empty-handed.

"You ought to take a picture with me, David," she says now. "It'll probably be the last one you get."

My mother's always been to the point like that. She used to like to say that she was "blunt," seemed proud of that fact.

"You can put it on Facebook," she says. "I don't really care."

My mother lived mostly off-the-grid in a rundown house in Mississippi: no TV, no car, just a bunch of old mildewed books and newspapers and magazines, so I don't know how she even knows what Facebook is, but that's my mother: full of mysteries and surprises.

So, I stand next to where she lay in the hospital bed, plastic tubes coming from her side, a blood pressure cuff inflating and deflating against the flaked skin of her arm, producing red and green numbers on a black screen beside where I'm crouching next to her—a constant beep and hiss signaling the sounds of her life—and then I lean down close so my daughter can take a picture of us together.

My mother finally tells me happy birthday before we all have to leave a few hours later.

Seventh Picture: *My father and me, in my kitchen, 2019*
There's a birthday cake in front of us. I'm turning thirty-nine and in four days, my father will be seventy-one. It's the first birthday we've spent together like this. The first birthday we've spent together in our entire lives. Until just a short time ago, neither one of us knew the other existed.

But just yesterday, he flew down with his partner to meet my family and me. And we'll end up taking a lot more pictures together like this; in a few months, when we go to visit him at his home, which is over a thousand miles away from where I was born and was raised by a family who wasn't my own, we'll take plenty more. I'll keep them all in a photo album. It's the only way to make up for almost forty years of lost time, to preserve something of our relationship for my own kids one day. And for myself, of course. It's something tangible so that we'll all have a story to tell. Stories like this are so important: they can offer a faith in the human will to connect and to love.

Six months before this picture was taken, my mother passed away. She never knew that I found my father, and I wonder what she would think about all this now. Would she be sad, embarrassed, happy? I have to be honest and say that I don't really know the answer to that question.

Eighth Picture: *My mother, my father, and me, standing outside, 1990*
This is a picture that doesn't exist: it's of me, my mother, and my father, all together. The three of us. Maybe we're all smiling, maybe they're holding hands—my parents—and we're standing in a nice yard, in front of a nice house, and there's a dog in it, too. Why not? I'm ten years old. Younger than my own kids are now.

Of course, I'm imagining these things.

The clouds are thick and full overhead, and all the shadows and light are so remarkable that the picture comes out perfect. It's one of those rare moments, the kind you would frame and put on a shelf. It's a photograph that people would ask you about.

"Is this you?" they'd say, lifting the picture up to examine it, touching the glass with their finger.

"Yeah," you'd say. "That was a while ago though." And you'd think: *Jesus, time flies.*

"Wow," they'd say. "I can't believe how much you look like your parents." Or something to that effect.

"I know," you'd say. "It's incredible, isn't it?"

Then, they'd put the picture down on the shelf and move on to something else in your house, this place you've worked so hard to make for your family.

But you might stay behind for a second longer though. Look at the photograph again, notice a glint of light in the frame that you hadn't caught until now—how it makes everything seem almost real for a minute. Alive.